RAISE YOUR ROOF

RAISE
YOUR ROOF

THE HIDDEN POWER
OF YOUR POTENTIAL

KARL SUBBAN
WITH ELLE GLENCOE

Collins

An Imprint of HarperCollins Publishers

Published by HarperCollins Publishers Ltd

First edition

HarperCollins books may be purchased for educational, business, or sales promotional use through our Special Markets Department.

HarperCollins Publishers Ltd
Bay Adelaide Centre, East Tower
22 Adelaide Street West, 41st Floor
Toronto, Ontario, Canada
M5H 4E3

www.harpercollins.ca

Library and Archives Canada Cataloguing in Publication

Title: Raise your roof : the hidden power of your potential / Karl Subban
    with Elle Glencoe.
Names: Subban, Karl, author. | Glencoe, Elle, author.
Description: First edition. | Includes bibliographical references.
Identifiers: Canadiana (print) 20240523849 | Canadiana (ebook)
    20240523849 | ISBN 9781443473446 (hardcover) |
    ISBN 9781443473453 (Ebook)
Subjects: LCSH: Self-actualization (Psychology) | LCSH: Change
    (Psychology) | LCSH: Goal (Psychology) | LCGFT: Self-help
    publications.
Classification: LCC BF637.S4 S866 2025 | DDC 158.1—dc23

Printed in the United States
24 25 26 27 28 LBC 5 4 3 2 1

Believe what the eyes see, verify what the mind believes, and centre your heart in your work.

CONTENTS

Introduction 1

PART I: THE POTENTIAL YOU
Chapter 1: The Man Without a Roof 9
Chapter 2: Look Up 18
Chapter 3: Light Your Flame 29

PART II: THE DREAMING YOU
Chapter 4: What Is a Dream? 43
Chapter 5: Unlabel Yourself 54
Chapter 6: Define Your Own Needs 64
Chapter 7: Become a Dream Leader 75

PART III: THE BELIEVING YOU
Chapter 8: What Is Believing? 85
Chapter 9: Trust Yourself to Fall 96
Chapter 10: Feel Safe Within 105
Chapter 11: Say Yes to Yourself 115
Chapter 12: Dig Deep Roots 126

PART IV: THE DOING YOU
Chapter 13: What Is Doing? 139
Chapter 14: Love the Game 151
Chapter 15: Throw Rocks with Strangers 159
Chapter 16: Do What You're Doing 170
Chapter 17: Taking the Right Course 180
Chapter 18: Start to Finish 191

PART V: THE MAGIC YOU
Chapter 19: Be the Mirror   203
Chapter 20: Shimmer like Gold   213
Chapter 21: Up and Beyond   225

Acknowledgements   229
Appendix: Raise Their Roof   231
Notes   239

INTRODUCTION

In *Outliers: The Story of Success*, author Malcolm Gladwell suggests that it takes 10,000 hours to become an expert in anything, to truly reach one's potential.[1] I'm sure you've heard about this idea at some point since Gladwell published his book in 2008. That figure is one that gets repeated over and over again in other books, on television programs, and even in schools.

As someone who coaches and teaches for a living, I'm naturally driven to understand what makes us better at who we are and what we do. When I first read about those 10,000 hours, I thought about my kids' hockey and basketball practices and the amount of time that went into their skills training, and I accepted that figure at face value.

At the same time, I wondered where Gladwell had acquired his numbers, and I started to dig. After all, getting the facts right is important.

When I read up on recent research about goal achievement, I found out that Gladwell's rule of thumb is actually a complete and total myth. In fact, there's a whole book called *Peak: Secrets from the New Science of Expertise* by Anders Ericsson and Robert Pool that demonstrates that a lot of people reach their potential without coming close to spending that amount of time getting ready.[2] Ericsson is an internationally renowned psychologist and researcher and, as he and science writer Pool write, our bodies and minds are highly adaptable, and we suffer under repetitive conditions. We reach our potential not by doing the same thing for a number of hours, but by honing our skills doing new things, more challenging things, and discovering what drives us.

All of this means that we don't have to create a countdown clock to success. We don't have to track our hours like we track our daily steps on an app. Ten thousand is not a magic number.

We can reach our potential if we just step up and step into our own lives.

We are constantly meeting new people, using new technologies, being exposed to new ideas, and moving from place to place. That means we are primed to grow, and we are primed to be the best version of ourselves.

We don't have to believe that we have all of the answers in life.

What we do have to believe is that we have the potential to find our path forward in a way that is meaningful for each of us.

In my life so far, I have had three major roles. You may already know me as a father because I've been lucky enough to raise five fantastic children, all of whom have served their communities and spent time in the public eye. Because of my children's success, I'm often asked how our family achieved our goals. I've learned many important lessons about helping children reach their potential, which I have enjoyed sharing in my books, interviews, and talks over the years.

You may not know that my professional role for closing in on forty years has been that of teacher and principal. I've been responsible not only for raising children at home but also for bringing up children in the community. A principal at both public and private schools, I have had the privilege of nurturing the potential of thousands of young people over the course of my career.

The evolution of this work has resulted in my professional transformation into a new role: that of public speaker and coach. This book, in some ways, is the culmination of many years of codifying what I have learned about what makes people tick, what makes them happy and content with their paths in life, and what allows them to feel authentically aligned with the potential they were born with.

In each of my roles, I have been passionately curious about how people reach their own potential.

I've learned that children don't just do what we tell them to do. They do what they *see us do*. They follow the pathways we create. Then, when we tell children that they can reach their potential and provide them with the support they need to believe it, they follow through. Time and again, I've witnessed children with the most challenging family lives and personal issues flourish and thrive, just because they believed in themselves.

Children are full of potential, but so are adults. We follow the same pathways we were introduced to as children. We get stuck in the same patterns we've seen in our own lives. And we also have the ability to dream big dreams, believe in our potential, and do what we need to get to where we want to be. We're no different from children. The same rules apply to every one of us.

Through my study of the human experience, I've learned that we can get unstuck from life and reach our highest goals.

Through all of this thing called "living life," the one constant that I have noticed is the power of potential. Our potential decides how we would like life to play out, how we would like the experience of living to feel, where we want to explore, and how we would like to take action.

All of us have the power to choose to reach our potential.

I know it doesn't always seem that we can reach our potential. More often, it feels like we have to follow a certain path lined with responsibilities to others, predetermined guidelines and activities, and daily timelines. Most of us don't remember that we have the power to reach our potential, not just some of the time but all of the time. It certainly does not always *feel* that way. Because I have watched so many individuals reach their potential, I know this to be true: it is wholly attainable to every one of us.

But for some of us, we have forgotten that to reach our potential is our birthright. It always has been. How can we begin to remember?

Given that we are already good at making changes in our lives, choosing to reach our potential shouldn't be all that difficult. After all, in this book, I'm going to show you exactly how to reach your potential. And I'm going to break it down into easy steps and exercises that will allow each of you to reach your potential with ease, grace, and awareness.

The first part of this book is called The Potential You. In it, I'm going to talk about what potential really means and how you may have faced real or imagined barriers to reaching it in the past. Why? Because before we get into methods of reaching your potential, you'll need to unpack some of the reasons you may not have achieved your goals before now. By understanding more about yourself and what your roadblocks may be, you'll be better prepared to move forward with confidence and clarity.

Next comes The Dreaming You. In this second part of the book, you'll work out what your authentic life dream is and how that dream can start you on your way to reaching your potential. Being able to identify what matters to you, deep down, will allow you to set a plan in motion.

The third part of the book is called The Believing You. Often, our biggest challenge isn't coming up with a dream, but rather believing enough in our own potential that we take steps to see our goals through to completion. This part leads you through exercises that make believing in yourself easier so that you can get the support you need to follow your dreams.

The Doing You takes you through your action path to reaching your potential. This fourth part helps you define the steps you need to take and the practices you should incorporate into your life so that your belief turns into present-day reality.

Finally, in The Magic You, all of the lessons are drawn together into an inspirational framework for your future development as a living, loving, and successful human being. Potential is magic because with it, you can reach more, do more, and become more. Potential is the beauty that we each possess inside of us.

I know that you can reach your potential.

Do you?

Because this book is not about me, nor my opinions.

This book is about you.

In this book, I won't be telling you what reaching your potential should look like. I can't decide what a life well lived looks like for you.

In fact, the term "personal growth" feels like a burden for that very reason. How do we define our own personal growth? It seems, to most people, that being on a journey towards personal growth is about living your best life. But what is "best"?

My gift to you is to reflect back those ideas, values, and skills that are already inside you.

My gift is to remind you that you are so brilliant and so wonderful, right here and now.

My gift is to help you begin to recognize and remember your own potential.

PART I

THE POTENTIAL YOU

CHAPTER 1

The Man Without a Roof

An Old Man lived in a small one-room house that was starved for furniture and material things. He had spent his life serving people as a carpenter, building things to fit their needs. His customers' vision became his life's mission. He was a good, caring, and trusted builder, which made him very busy and popular across his community.

His one-room house had one small door, a small bed for resting his head at night, and a table with a pile of books standing in one corner. The one-room house had one colossal window, which furnished the house with fresh air and sunlight.

On the floor, sitting below the window, was a bucket filled with soil to the rim.

Just below the soil's surface, the Old Man had planted one lonely seed.

In the seed, the man saw the enormous potential. He saw a tall, beautiful tree decorated with the prettiest flowers in bloom. The man was sad for the lonely seed because he knew that it would never see its own flower in the season of bloom. On the other hand, he was happy that it would serve its life's purpose.

When it became a tiny plant sitting in the big, big bucket, it was so small, it could barely be seen. The plant's place in the room was closest to the only window so it could receive the most sunlight, and the man called the plant Grow.

The man was never lonely living with Grow, and the plant was not growing alone in the one-room house. The small plant received his attention, nourishment, and enrichment as the man watered and cared for the plant daily.

Over time, the man was delighted to see Grow's growth and development.

Over many weeks, it reached just below the height of the window.

Then, Grow was the same height as the window.

Until one day, it was even taller than the Old Man.

The man was delighted to see the physical change in the plant. It had grown many more branches. The leaves grew more prominent with a deeper, richer colour of green.

The plant started small, but it grew tall, taller and taller until it reached the ceiling of the one-room house. It could not go any higher or further because of one big obstacle: the roof.

The Old Man did not know what to do to help Grow grow some more. A change was needed, but he did not know what steps to take. He saw the roof and the problem but did not have a solution.

But then, everything changed as he stared at the ceiling above him.

He knew one thing: plants were made to grow, and Grow was no exception.

The plant had the potential to grow more, which meant that the Old Man had to do more. The man contemplated several options:

He could allow the plant to grow to the maximum height of the ceiling, which would limit its potential.

He could cut or prune the plant.

He could build another room with no roof for the plant to grow into the world.

He could make a hole in the roof for the plant to grow through and find its own way.

He could raise the roof for the plant, and for himself.

After studying his options, the Old Man decided to raise the roof of his one-room house. He used what he was good at doing to help the plant grow to its potential. He was a carpenter who built things. A good carpenter builds things for people. But the best ones solve problems to create the best things for people. He was good at building things, so his very best option was to raise the roof for the plant to grow some more.

One morning, after waking up and looking up at Grow now growing under its new raised roof, he saw the prettiest flower he had ever seen. Perching on the top of the flower was a beautiful butterfly. It had made Grow its home. While looking through and beyond the plant framed in the window opening, the Old Man saw the prettiest rainbow in the morning sky.

The Old Man smiled big that morning because he saw his life story in nature's treasures: the plant, butterfly, and rainbow. The rainbow represented his desires, dreams, and the goals he had been reaching for, once too far away. Now he knew and believed that, deep inside him, he had the wings of the butterfly to go places and do things he never thought possible. Learning and working to be the carpenter he was made to be required him to raise his roof to reach his abilities. He was blooming in life when he completed the projects that his customers wanted, and also in his state of mind, knowing he did his best in all he did.

Raising the roof of the one-room house was all the plant needed to grow, blossom, and bloom. Something had had to change for Grow to grow into its *potential*.

What does the word *potential* mean? It's the essence of the moment when we start dreaming about something magical that we alone can bring into being. Potential is something we all have inside of us, but we haven't put it into action yet. Potential energy, for example, is the energy that is stored inside our bodies in the form of calories, waiting to be released as we take one step forward from the starting line. *Potential growth*, another example, is the innate ability we have to get bigger, to build our communities, or to create a business that makes money once we put a plan in motion.

What does the word *potential* mean? It's the essence of the moment when we start dreaming about something magical that we alone can bring into being.

When we change, we grow. And when we grow, we change. It's a cyclical, circular personal process that helps us tap into our own ability to see opportunities, possibilities, and pathways in front of us.

When we raise the roof under which we are living, working, learning, or playing, we, too, will grow and blossom and bloom. That's how we reach our potential. We never know how far we can go until we give ourselves more room to recognize and realize who we are.

Potential is our capacity for making changes, whether or not we choose to use that capacity.

What do I mean by this?

Everyone has the potential to take on their dream job, building the skills and the know-how to live out our passion in life.

Everyone has the potential to find solace and peace, creating a home that soothes and comforts us every night.

Everyone has the potential to build knowledge, taking on a new intellectual challenge.

Everyone has the potential to travel, exploring what lies outside of our comfort zone.

Everyone has the ability to grow, but as the story of the old man teaches us, it may not be that simple.

Sure, a big part of us naturally matures as we get older. Even so, that only means we're getting bigger, not necessarily better. Many of us fear that we will not reach our potential before we get too old to realistically achieve all our goals. Many of us fear that we have old psychological blocks in the way, preventing us from reaching our potential even if we had the skills to do so.

To understand ourselves as adults, it pays to understand ourselves as kids.

As a principal at Brookfield Middle School in the Jane Finch neighbourhood of Toronto, known for its high level of socioeconomic strain, I would ask a roomful of students a simple question: "Anyone who wants to be better, will you raise your hand?"

Every hand shot up. That came as no surprise. Who doesn't want to be better? Everybody wants to be better. Everyone wants to grow into their potential.

The problem was that too many children didn't think they could be any better than they were right at that moment. They couldn't see the roof, let alone raise it.

The same is true for every adult, and not just those in Jane Finch. You, like everyone you know, has a picture in your head of what it looks and feels like to reach your potential, but you don't necessarily believe that your dreams are going to become actualized.

In fact, instead of betting on ourselves, we often bet on other people. I myself have looked to others as leaders: not only to hockey players like Ken Dryden, but also to thought leaders like Brené Brown and John Maxwell. Each of us have our own heroes in life: sports stars, inspirational and spiritual leaders, actors and other performers, writers and directors, and more. My own son, PK, has been an inspiration to many as a hockey defenceman, but also as a philanthropist and sports journalist.

We all look up to those who have travelled paths before us. Of course, we're going to be inspired by people who work to make their lives better and, sometimes, change the world in the process. It's what psychologist Leon Festinger termed "upward social comparison" in 1954. People compare themselves to those who are better than them, in some small or significant way, when they want inspiration to improve. It's a means to jog our imagination for solutions and a push to ensure that we keep a goal in mind.

But sometimes, upward social comparison has a downside. Research shows that we might actually feel worse about ourselves when we look upward, because we think we can never meet our idols on their level.[1] We fear that other people can achieve their goals but we can't, for some hidden set of reasons, reasons that we fail to identify. In our minds, we separate ourselves from those who didn't settle for an everyday life because it feels better to think that they had a special gift, a special talent, more money, or more power. Instead of looking for a blueprint to success, we lift other people onto pedestals without recognizing all of the actions they took to step up on those pedestals all by themselves.

But my son PK did not win Olympic gold because my wife and I bought him some hockey skates.

Brené did not become a bestselling author because someone handed her a pen and a piece of paper.

I didn't become a school principal because I liked chalkboards.

For PK, for Brené, and for you and for me, the real trick is that we not only have to *allow* ourselves to grow, we have to create the conditions in which growth is possible.

I'm not asking you to believe in yourself right now. That's actually a difficult thing to accomplish.

So often, we hear that same bland call to action: "Believe in yourself!" The problem with that command is that there are actually many legitimate and life-challenging barriers to believing that you can do something goal-oriented with your life right now. There are, in fact, *so many* of these barriers that we're going to talk about them in the next chapter of this book.

Instead, I am asking you to believe in your own *potential*.
Think about it this way:

▶ We don't know how many medical students are going to
  graduate to become doctors.
▶ We don't know how many people who write blogs will also
  write published books.
▶ We don't know how many law students will become lawyers.
▶ We don't know how many people who go to an art class at
  their local community centre will become recognized for their
  creations.
▶ We don't know how many soccer players will make it to the
  professional ranks.

We're never going to know until time passes and life plays out.
But no matter what goals these folks are trying to reach, they have
a lot in common. What are the three things that are the same about
all these people?

1. They are all working towards their *dreams*.
2. They are all *trying* to do something that they haven't done
   before.
3. They all have the potential to do these things *eventually*.

They may not have become the best in their field yet. They may
not have even conquered the basics of their field. But they've set
a dream in motion, they're trying, and it is possible that they will
get there. If they don't do 1 and 2 on this list, 3 will never come
true.

Think about that for a moment: 1 and 2 on this list are necessary
for 3 to be possible. We'll come back to that later in this book.

No matter what, your path forward starts with letting go of core beliefs about what to expect from yourself. Your potential is all about imagining the possibilities that intrigue you, that drive you, that, if you accomplished them, would make you feel like a better you.

So, for right now, I'm not going to ask you to set any goals. Instead, start by asking yourself some core questions.

1. When it comes to your personal growth and development, how much time and effort are you willing to give?
2. What is one thing that you can change today to feel a little bit better about yourself?
3. If you were the old man in the story, what decision would you have made to clear the way for the plant to grow to its full potential?
4. Are you comfortable under your roof? Are you a roof-buster?
5. What steps are you taking to learn, grow, and develop past your roof?

Never underestimate a person living in a house with no roof. I'm not going to be the one to tell anyone that they have to have a roof, because, more often than not, I've seen what happens when people remember that they can change their trajectory. I've seen what happens when people raise that roof or simply get rid of it altogether.

I've seen people meet their potential. And blow right past it. And I'm so happy for them when that happens.

As a principal, I talk to all of my students in their classrooms every year, and I ask them to say one phrase. I ask them to repeat that phrase over and over again until they feel it in their hearts. I do the same thing when I work with adults in leadership roles who have lost their commitment or don't know what to do next. It's a powerful phrase because it's all about your personal power.

It's time for you to say those six magic words: "I believe in my own potential."

I'm not kidding. Say those words out loud. "I believe in my own potential."

Say them again! "I believe in my own potential."

You may not be where you want to be on your life's path. You may not even believe in those six words as you say them aloud. Not yet. Each person's potential is realized at a different place on their life journey than everyone else's.

In the next chapter, we're going to talk about why we perceive barriers to raising the roof. In fact, these barriers aren't just perceived, they are sometimes very substantial. We may not even realize that we have barriers in our way. But I want you to keep in mind that these barriers are not too high for you to climb. Like Grow, you can weave your way around barriers to find your way to the rooftops.

No matter what, you have to know that your potential lies inside of you, ready to be released. There's something reminding you of that right now, in your own mind. And if not, I'm reminding you instead.

Your power is your potential.

What's stopping you from raising your roof?

CHAPTER 2

Look Up

Roger Bannister became the first person to run a mile in under four minutes. That race took place in May 1954 during a meet between British AAA and Oxford University at Iffley Road Track in Oxford, with only British participants. But only forty-six days later, in June, Bannister's record was broken by his Australian rival, John Landy, in Turku, Finland. That's why, when the 1954 British Empire and Commonwealth Games launched in Vancouver in August, the world knew that it was going to be a close race. The papers were billing the standoff as the "Miracle Mile."

Landy led for most of the race. In fact, he had gained a solid lead of 10 yards by the third lap out of the four required. Bannister was doing his best to catch up. And then Landy made his fatal mistake. He looked over his left shoulder to see where the rest of the runners were, and as he did so, Bannister passed him on his right.

It's at the turning point in any endeavour that you have to keep looking forward.

It's just like riding a bike. When you're turning a corner on a bicycle, if you don't look where you're aiming to head, you'll fall down. You have to lean into the turn and keep your focus on the road or you'll end up sliding off the pavement.

To raise your roof, you need the same kind of forward focus. What's right in front of you?

And you can't look too far ahead, either. Very recently, I got into a fender bender. It was about 6:45 in the evening, and as it was still the dregs of winter, it was dark outside. I remember approaching the red light, but there were six or seven cars stopped ahead of me. They were waiting for the light to turn green, as was I. The moment I saw green, I put my foot on the gas. But the driver in front of me did not, and I didn't notice. I bumped right into him because I was overfocused on my own goal of getting home faster, just like Landy.

But why don't we all learn how to set goals and focus on what's ahead of us? The simplified answer is that many people don't give themselves permission to imagine and move towards the future they actually want, and so they learn to settle for less.

The more complicated answer is that there is a combination of psychological and neurological patterns that can bind to the social experiences that shape us.[1] As an educator, I've witnessed this in my students: there is no divide between nature and nurture, as both come into play simultaneously. There are no intrinsically bad children; there are only children with better or worse support systems. Even children with mental health disorders can thrive, given the right support. But our life patterns and experiences stick together like glue and become a map to our own personal world in our brains. Even though we're all capable of change, these synaptic maps are often difficult to shift. We have to work hard to help ourselves, and each other, to build new inroads into our thoughts and behaviours.

We don't have a people problem, we have a *potential* problem. Life is a bit like going into a drive-through at Tim Hortons or McDonald's. Before you make it to the order window, there's an Enter Here sign, and a Do Not Enter sign. You don't want to go the wrong way because you're going to get hurt. But, many days, you're on autopilot or you're not thinking clearly because you're stressed out. When you see those signs, that voice in your head gets muddled and echoes for a moment. Sometimes you make it into the right lane, sometimes you slow down and get honked at from behind, and sometimes you just decide to haphazardly park the car instead.

The same messy, doubting feeling also takes place when you lose sight of yourself and your potential and you ask yourself, "Which way should I go? Where am I allowed to go next?"

You know that echoing voice in your head. That's where the doubt lives.

"I can't do it. I'm not bright enough. I'm not smart enough. I'm not white enough. I'm not good enough. I'm not tall enough. I'm not pretty enough."

When you finally get to the order window, someone asks you, "What do you want?"

In life, you're asked, "What do you want to be? What do you want to become?"

At the pickup window, what must you do before they give you what you ordered? You have to pay the price. You have to pay for your double-double or your Big Mac.

In your own personal growth story, you also have to pay for what you want: in sweat, in tears, and in time and sometimes money.

The real challenge you're going to face in life is that it's a lot harder to imagine your future path forward than it is to figure out how to buy a coffee on a bad day. But the same tenet applies: if you feel upset or pressurized or worried about money or your family or your job, the entire transaction may feel overwhelming, or it might not work at all.

Focusing on the goal we set for ourselves is the goal that we will eventually achieve. When you take your eyes off the prize entirely, or you're looking to skip all the steps you need to move forward effectively, you end up losing the race. You have the ability to raise your roof by learning to fight distractions and not let anyone else's performance affect your choices.

> We don't have a people problem,
> we have a *potential* problem.

The first step to raising your roof is to forgive yourself for not believing in your own dreams, at least not yet. It's critical to understand the external barriers you might be facing. There are many things that stand in the way of our personal growth, development, and momentum, so much so that the roof above us blocking our growth seems to be made of brick and stone. External blocks include how we were raised and educated, our environment and community, and the voices and opinions of the people with whom we spend our time. These are issues that have nothing to do with who we choose to become and everything to do with the people, places, and ideas we were exposed to as children and that we may still be facing today.

These blocks exist. They are real. They are heavy burdens for each of us to carry. It is okay to take time to chip away at them or to allow others to help us lift them.

Together, I want us to recognize and name these blocks so that your experiences can be seen and heard, and so that you understand you're not alone in your feelings. It makes sense that you're worried you're never going to become the person you want to be. And once you truly know that, we can clear the way.

The way I count them, there are **five external issues** that might stand in our way and five possible pathways to help us move beyond these issues.

• **Trauma.** Everyone has their own life story, and, for far too many of us, trauma, fear, and adversity go hand in hand. When we experience trauma in childhood, whether at home or in our community, it doesn't only have mental health implications: it can change our physiology, especially our nervous systems.[2] In schools, we have a tool called the Adverse Childhood Experience (ACE) checklist[3] that helps us assess whether or not our students are dealing with active trauma. What our profession has discovered is that ACEs are very, very common. About 64 percent of adults have reported they had experienced at least one type of ACE before age eighteen, and more than one in six (17.3 percent) reported they had experienced four or more types of ACEs.[4] ACE-related health consequences cost an estimated economic burden of $748 billion annually in Bermuda, Canada, and the United States.[5] We can't deny that we have had these experiences, and, even more so, we must acknowledge them because trauma can only be set aside; it does not ever leave us entirely. *Acknowledging our trauma can mean getting mental or physical health support and social support, or, at the very least, giving ourselves the gift of emotional awareness and self-forgiveness for our fear and upset.*

• **Environment.** The community we live in, and its physical, natural environment, can have an effect on us. Think about hermit crabs for a moment. Sometimes, they might be stuck with a poor-fitting shell. If it's too large or too small or too heavy, it can cause them to die. These crabs leave their inhospitable shells. Likewise, sometimes we ought to leave our own social or geographical environment due to stress and strain. But there are times when we can't follow our instincts due to economic or family pressure. *Even if we can't leave our homes or communities, we have to remember that we're still growing inside, and we can place our focus there.*

• **Parenting.** Despite the fact that we're adults, the parenting we received as children will always affect us, even if we don't experience family trauma. Sometimes, parents don't see that their child has dreams, feelings, and desires of their own. Sometimes, parents restrict a child's perspective on the world in trying to keep them safe. Parents may push their child towards what they want that child to become, rather than recognizing a young person's own point of view on their future. *If our parents haven't served us well, we have to learn as adults how to make space for our own beliefs and values and discover what we love on our own.*

• **Health.** Our mental and physical well-being can feel like a huge block, especially if we are affected by a condition that is chronic or beyond our control. Our health, if it is not in working order, has a significant impact on our time. It takes longer to get things done. It means that we have to rest more often. We have to recognize our limitations more overtly. Dopamine positively affects our senses of pleasure, satisfaction, and motivation. When you feel good that you've achieved something, it's because you have a surge of dopamine in the brain. *When we are negatively affected by health issues, it is an invitation to pay more attention to our own desires, dreams, and potential, because with this kind of self-care comes the release of dopamine.*

• **Education.** An education will help you to make it *through* life, not make it *in* life. An education is not just a certification checkbox, and it's not just a piece of paper. There are many of us who don't spend time on our education because we believe that it won't make us money in the future. That's true! A degree doesn't mean a better salary in many fields. But when our parents or our friends convince us that we won't benefit from learning, that's not true. *Lifelong learning is something that we can provide to ourselves, whether through a degree, a course, or lived experience, and we should embrace every opportunity we have to learn.*

There are internal blocks as well, like our own habits and mindsets, our personalities and attitudes, that act as barriers to our potential. Despite the heaviness of external blocks, internal blocks may be even harder to shift. That's because many of these are blocks that we've lifted into place by ourselves.

The following list includes five internal barriers that we create for ourselves. Every one of these barriers is our personal responsibility to fix.

• **Mindset.** Carol Dweck talks about why a growth mindset versus a fixed mindset is so important.[6] As she writes, a growth mindset is not about making more of an effort. It's about learning from the process, knowing you'll be in a new situation, and growing from the changes. A fixed mindset is different. A fixed mindset happens when you get "stuck" in the same situation, telling the same stories over and over again. You have the ability to look at a problem and tell yourself that it can't be fixed, or you can find a new story. You can tell yourself that this is a challenge, an adventure, or a new opportunity that you're excited to explore. *Remember, your mind is powerful, and you can replace excuses with ambition.*

• **Belief.** One of my favourite books, *The Very Hungry Caterpillar* by Eric Carle, is an iconic story of a small insect whose journey from egg to butterfly is a metaphor for personal growth. The caterpillar was chasing a dream, and he had hope that he could change himself into something extraordinary. *Decide that an open mind is a gold mine, and find space in your life for imagination and creativity.*

• **Friendships.** Friendship is so important. It represents the principles of flight: it can lift you up, thrust you forward, or drag you down. People can introduce gravity into your life, especially if you end up carrying them. They can also introduce you to new ideas, values, and circumstances where you can explore possibility. Friendships can also become serious distractions or detractors from your goals. If you are spending time on someone else's schedule, goals, and missions, then you're not spending it building your own potential. *You can't change the people around you, but you can change who you choose to be around.*

• **Character.** Your DNA and your environment might frame who you are. But the choices you make determine your character. Even if we have mental health issues, we have some control over our character and the decisions we make to put time into our own personal growth. The way we develop over time is so important to who we become. Our character, and by this I also mean our integrity and sense of responsibility for our own future, shapes every part of who we are. What words would friends use to describe you as a person? How are you making people feel? *Even if you're not ready to be the best at something yet, it's your responsibility to be the better version of yourself.*

• **Routine.** John Maxwell has taught that our agenda today tells everyone who we are going to be tomorrow. Your routine tells me how bad you want something. If you are doing something every day, that's going to shape how good you become at that particular skill or task. Are you just "busy" or are you taking intentional steps towards your goals? *Your routine and your habits need to be supporting a bigger mission in life.*

Look up and see what's in your way.

You have some blocks. I have some blocks. I am giving you permission to set your burdens aside. Whether your blocks are external, internal, or both, they are a huge barrier to raising your roof.

You are not a problem. Ever. You are wonderful. You are your own future.

We all have barriers; we can't let them be a problem. We can't let them stop us.

But if you have even one of the previous ten barriers (external and internal) to realizing your potential, you have to measure it, understand it, and start to think about how to remove it. Bringing awareness to your blocks is the first step. Once you know you have a block, what do you do to break it down?

There are some clues in the entries above, but I'm also going to challenge you to look at all of the clues together and discover what they're telling you. Bring these ideas into clarity, because they come down to one simple question: Where are you placing your focus?

If you spend all the time focusing on the problem, it becomes you. You are not a prisoner to your DNA or to the environment or to your parents. You are learning, playing, living, and working right now. Every moment you breathe, you have potential to change what happens next.

We can allow these blocks to make our lives bitter, or we can give ourselves permission to make our lives better.

Don't look down.

Look up.

Simon Sinek, the author of *Start with Why*,[7] says to begin by asking why some people might be more successful than others. But he might be making things a bit more complex than they need to be, and he might be missing out on the foibles of human nature. Not everyone wakes up with a "why" in mind, and we may not want to. We don't have to tie up everything in a neat package and figure it all out at once to have potential. If you're not doing something with your time, you're not going to discover what you're capable of becoming next. That's a situation where your roof is so low that you're crouched on the ground.

So let's start with some easier things:

- ▶ What are your interests? Cooking, photography, nature, helping people? Everyone has an interest. Give yourself permission to take a class or volunteer.
- ▶ Find a book that you might love to read, about absolutely any topic, take it out from the library, and read it.
- ▶ Write lists of what you like, love, want, and need. Explore the difference between these lists. What does that feel like?
- ▶ Try literally bouncing off the walls if it feels good (and if it's safe). Or try painting those walls, colouring your world.
- ▶ Pay attention to the small things that you love doing.

Where are you placing your focus?

Some people wonder why they keep ending up in the same place in life, but they haven't figured out they should be taking a different road. If you don't start by noticing what you want and love, and who you imagine yourself to be, you won't be able to plan your next steps on any road.

There is no need to test your potential. If you are like any one of my students, I know your potential has been tested too many times to count.

You might not have done everything just quite yet, and that is okay.

You might not know your "why."

You may have had a lot of blocks holding you down.

But you're still here, and if you're reading this book, you're ready.

In the next chapter, we'll explore the story of one person I know who felt that her potential was being tested and what she did about it. We'll talk about why we are burning the candle at both ends and how we can make small changes in our lives that shift the way we see our potential futures.

No matter what, as we go through the exercises in this book, I want you to remember to trust in your potential.

And don't forget to look up. Little by little, you'll see your roof being raised.

CHAPTER 3

Light Your Flame

One day, I was speaking to a good friend, Maria, who felt like she was locked into a difficult work and life schedule. Not just sometimes, but most of the time.

"Karl, my job is very demanding," she said to me. "I need your help to figure this out. I'm on a new project every couple of months, and sometimes I get a call to start on a client project the day I'm finishing the last one. I am pushing myself so hard because I need to support my family, not just at home but also my grandparents back in Indonesia who count on me to send them money."

"Are you meeting your own high standards?" I asked her. "Or are you just following the roles and rules set out for you by other people?"

"Well, kind of both," Maria admitted. "I love being a technology specialist. I'm proud of the fact that I am the kind of consultant who can demand a significant hourly and daily fee. I know that, usually, I am very energized by my work and the sense of accomplishment I feel, and I feel financially successful as well. But I don't feel right with myself, and to some extent, I don't feel right with my family, either. I feel like I'm not spending enough time with either my kids in Toronto or my grandparents back in Jakarta, especially since we live so far away from each other."

"Why do you think that is the case? What do you think isn't adding up?"

"Every project I take on is a chance to up my rate, to gain the confidence of people with power and connections, and to create greater career opportunities. That's not necessarily a bad thing, focusing on and having a successful career. I think it's good for my children to see me being successful as well. But I know that not everything I'm doing is actually connected to what I really want to do in my heart."

"What do you think that is, my friend?"

"I think it's because I just keep going from one project to the next, and when I look back at how I have spent my time, I end up having to face my limitations. And the biggest limitation that I am facing is the fact that I'm too tired to really enjoy my own life and the success that I've created for myself and my family."

"I want you to think about this next question carefully. What's the biggest hurdle you're facing right now to having that enjoyment?"

"Time. I feel like it's slipping away. I feel like if I had more time, I could rekindle my flame, my joy in life."

"Well, you say that you're in demand and your consulting rate is rising. What if you built in time at the beginning and end of projects so that you didn't have to be accountable to anyone, say, for one week before and after?"

"Take time off? Karl, people call me up and I have to be ready to go. My tech consultant friends would be horrified at the very idea of taking extended breaks between contracts. But it's more than that. I grew up poor, and I know I have to hustle if I'm going to survive, especially as a single mom."

I thought hard about Maria's perceived problem. I noted that what she was talking about was a physical survival strategy. She wasn't talking about a simple scheduling issue. Maria couldn't see the difference between the two, because she was anxious.

That's what I brought to her attention: Maria wasn't going to solve the problem at hand if she was actually, somewhere in her subconscious, worried about something else. I told her she'd already mastered staying alive and feeding her kids. Now, she had to raise her roof that little bit more and make room for herself.

Maria made a choice to build a week-long break between her next contracts, a buffer that stayed hidden in her own calendar. No one else had to know. She found that the positive impact on her life and how she was living it was unprecedented. All of a sudden, Maria had eight weeks of vacation to spend with her family every year. She still made sure she had that next contract lined up so she felt safe, but she confidently left her laptop in her office when she took that time for herself.

For years, my friend had bought into the idea that she had to answer every call to action.

Don't we all?

In some ways, Maria's story sounds all too familiar. The time stresses that we are likely to face balancing work and life mean that we are burning the candle at both ends. Not all of us have the kind of job that allows us to take time off and visit family overseas. But remember, Maria didn't think she did, either.

But it wasn't just the family time that mattered in this case.

Something else magical took place for Maria when she made this change in her schedule. For the first time in her adult life, she had the space to really be alone with herself.

Spending time alone with her thoughts did not feel magical at first; it simply felt *odd*. In fact, Maria wasn't actually sure what to do with herself when she was not working or on a more traditional family vacation.

The magic was that Maria started to remember things, things about herself and what was important to her.

Maria wanted to be able to make a positive impact on the world, and on the lives of children. She had seen that young people back in Indonesia needed support, and when she had the time to think and feel, Maria was finally able to *see* what was important to her. She started a technology program for kids back home, funded by her clients, friends, and her own work, and she developed a partnership with a non-profit education organization in Jakarta that helped to share the program with schools across the country.

Over time, the breaks in Maria's work and her family life, which increased both in frequency and duration, fuelled not only her own flame. She ended up inspiring others and building young people's belief in their own potential. Like Maria, we can all lose our flame when we forget that we are all free to change.

What happens in our lives when we don't recognize our inherent freedom to make choices that serve us? What happens if we remain tied to our own limited personal expectations, expectations based on some abstract goal with little to no real conscious choice for the rest of our lives? What do we have to lose in letting change happen?

> We can all lose our flame when we forget that we are all free to change.

Of course, our ingrained ideas of the survival of the fittest have a lot to do with the choices we make in our lives. We want to understand the behaviours that may help us and avoid those that have the potential to hurt us. We want to choose the safest path, even if that means overwork. We pursue relationships that superficially feel fulfilling. We look for patterns every day so that we can protect ourselves and, perhaps, move towards something more satisfying. For millennia, those of us who were good at recognizing threats tended to survive. The ability to be good at seeing patterns became a key survival skill, so it is not a surprise that this ability is prevalent and pervasive in most of us alive today.

But our life patterns that aren't related to immediate threats don't always get recognized. These patterns are invisible unless we create a way to see them, to take the time we need to become more aware of what patterns we are searching for and what we do with them once we find them.

If we want to come back to ourselves and stop burning the candle at both ends, then we need to see what we are *really* doing and *why* we are doing it.

Think about it: you can keep stubbing your toe running too fast, or you can make choices that allow you to feel your way towards personal growth in a more organic way.

Does this personal growth journey that you are on need to feel so hard and painful so frequently?

I think not.

In fact, I know it does not.

Potential is your starting line, not your finish line. That means that you're allowed to sit at the starting line for a moment in order to get yourself sorted on your life's journey.

At the starting line, it's time to realize that your potential is your seat, not your sneakers. Your potential is a three-legged stool, and each leg talks.

The first leg says: "You've got to be a dreamer."

The second leg says: "You've got to be a believer."

The third leg says: "You've got to be a doer."

Potential is your starting line, not your finish line.

All three of these identities are critical to reaching your potential. If any one of these legs is weak, the stool won't stand. When your stool is not right, it does not support the achievements and successes for which you were made. You and I will both fall when our stool of potential is not built strong enough to support us or when one of its legs crumbles. I'm not talking about the day-to-day tripping, stumbling, or falling short of a goal, that we all have when our schedule feels like a crunch, but the emotional fall we experience due to a circumstance out of our control, or even one within our control.

So what are these stool legs really talking about?

Leg 1. Dreaming is about awakening the spark of your potential.

Your dream should never be smaller than the life you are living today; it should be much, much bigger and grander. Your dream should be something that you can imagine doing, even if you don't know the path to get there yet. A dreamer has a vision of their own and isn't following someone else's path for their future.

I learned this lesson first-hand with one of my hockey-playing sons, Malcolm. I had trained him to play defence because he was one of the best players in his age group in the Greater Toronto Hockey League, the largest minor hockey league in the world. When I watched him play and observed his skills, I thought he loved to play that position. At one game, our team was down 4–1 going into the final period, and Malcolm scored three straight goals to help bring our team to victory. But a short time later, he shared with me that if he couldn't become a goalie, he would quit playing hockey. I was genuinely surprised to learn that, in Malcolm's eyes, he was living someone else's dream: my own. I immediately stepped out of his way. He became a goalie and is now living out his dream playing in the NHL.

To live a happy and productive life, it must be your dream that you are chasing. The dream in our heart is more powerful than the dreams that people have for us. Your dream gives you a sense of direction. You just never know how far you can go when the spark comes from within you, not from the outside.

Leg 2. Believing is about connecting to your potential and fanning the flame.

Believing is giving yourself permission to explore who you are. Imagining your future self in action strengthens your commitment.

In January 1958, Willie O'Ree became the first Black person to play in the NHL. The year is very significant to my story. It is important to me because I was born in 1958. I see it as more than a coincidence that I happened to be born at that time. I don't mind telling people that I was born to have a relationship with the sport. It was hockey that helped me more than anything else with my transition to Canada and believing in a new way of living. Hockey has transformational powers.

We all rise and fall in life based on our beliefs about our abilities to learn, grow, and develop. Willie believed that he would play in the NHL to live out his dream, even when the odds were not on his side. He believed a lot more in his abilities than he did in the odds working against him or the belief others had in him.

Willie broke important barriers, not only for himself, but for others. Exciting changes happen when rules and norms are broken and we don't do what we're supposed to do. In fact, the future of our world may depend on people feeling differently about what they allow themselves to do.

But the strength of your belief in your dreams will be tested. No one is excluded. I have told a story many times about PK playing in the well-known International Silver Stick minor hockey tournament. He walked out of his dressing room one day looking like something had died in him. When he came around emotionally, he told us what had happened in the room that was on rerun in his mind.

The coach had said, "PK, you will never make it in hockey or go as far as I did."

Whenever I share this story in my speaking engagements, I ask the audience if the coach's words stopped PK from believing in his NHL dream and imagining himself getting past this one experience. They always answer with a resounding no!

I often follow up with this question: "What is stopping you?"

Leg 3. Doing provides fuel for your internal fire.

A doer has the inspiration to act. Doing is unleashing your potential.

That's because, to reach your potential, you must be on the move.

"If you can't fly, run. If you can't run, walk. If you can't walk, crawl. But by all means keep moving,"[1] Martin Luther King Jr. reminds us. You must keep moving forward. You must move with a purpose and take many steps to act on your dream.

The future isn't something that happens to you, that you just stumble into. Instead, it is something you can create for yourself through your own determination and drive.

You have to take action.

If you are not taking any action at all, you will stagnate. I'm not saying this to make you feel guilty or make you work harder than you need to. But you, and everyone else on this planet, feels better when they have a purpose in life. When we forget about our purpose or we decide that we are too busy to follow that purpose, we feel smaller than we have to.

What would happen if we made absolutely no plans at all? In some ways, we would still be moving forward. In fact, every seven years, every cell in our body is replaced. Our brains are constantly changing as we grow and learn, building new neural pathways. We're becoming new versions of ourselves every day.

But when we are doers, we learn about the world or acquire new knowledge, and we're developing new perspectives on what we can do with our potential. Just making that small first step towards knowing and acting on your life's dream can make all the difference.

There is no system we learn that prepares us for life as it happens; we can only know ourselves and know that we can create the capacity to act on our dreams.

All of us want to be the heroes in our own lives.

We want to be successful.

We want others to look up to us.

We want to be the best at what we do.

In fact, if we are really honest with ourselves, we have to admit that we all want to be the best at everything!

But being the best at everything doesn't always apply, or make sense, or even matter. We don't have to be everyone's hero—not really, unless we are seeking to be the best version of ourselves. My best does not apply to you, and your best does not apply to me. That's why reaching our potential is the only thing we need to strive for in our lives.

So, as we move into the next part of the book, I want you to let go of all judgments of yourself. Over the rest of this book, in fact, we're going to undertake a series of you-centred exercises that will help you see your own potential.

All of us want to be the heroes in our own lives.

I try not to judge others. I've noticed that I really don't enjoy being judged by others, so it seems only right to choose not to judge them myself. But what is more important than this is the fact that we need to let go of self-judgment. We tend to seek out the comfort of judgment because life can just feel hard. Sometimes life *is* hard.

When you feel that life is getting difficult, remember three things.

1. You have already achieved so many things in life, hard things.
2. In seeking out personal growth by reading this book, you are doing better than yesterday.
3. Your best today could look very different from your best tomorrow, and you are always evolving.

In the same way, as you go through these exercises, you have to remember not to judge yourself. Remember, we tend to find what we seek.

Like Maria diligently looking for her next job rather than diligently looking for inspiration, we have to stop judging ourselves for not doing more. This judgment can become like an internal black hole, continuously drawing similar energies to ourselves. We all do this sometimes. I do this sometimes. But is this really the path to our potential? Are we really creating life in the way we would most love to?

Instead of doing more, we have to do better.

Personal growth can fire and inspire us, but it can also allow us the space to connect to our own ideas, values, needs, and desires.

In this world of high internal and external expectations, and where the demands only seem to grow more intense each day, we're simply tired. We're tired of traffic, of communication demands, of work overload, and, frankly, of ourselves. We live a life of disconnection from ourselves for the most part, and we don't get enough rest. We are exhausting ourselves fully and completely to the point where we may as well try something different.

For Maria, the minute she chose an energizing path, a path where she gave herself the space to make changes in her life, a green light switched on. Until she felt energized and available, the idea of personal growth really felt like a loaded and heavy invitation, and one that she felt unmotivated to take on.

So, as you go through the exercises in this book, remember that the option to simply make space is always available. You may not have the energy or time to do everything in this book in order, but you can take the time to think about what you are reading and let it resonate in your mind as you cook dinner, brush your teeth, or drive to work.

Simply being *with* yourself is the first step in awakening the spark inside you.

PART II

THE DREAMING YOU

CHAPTER 4

What Is a Dream?

When I was a little kid growing up in Jamaica, I wanted to be the famous West Indies cricketer Gary Sobers.

The man who would eventually be known as Sir Garfield St Aubrun Sobers was captain of the West Indies team from 1965 to 1972. This composite team of players are selected from a chain of fifteen English-speaking Caribbean nations. Sobers was not only an excellent sportsman but also a major part of a shift from a whites-only team to Black representation. Under Frank Worrell and then Sobers, the West Indies team would go on to be the strongest in the world in both Test and One Day International cricket in the 1970s and beyond.

Wanting to take after him, I needed my own cricket bat. In those days, we made our own.

I had heard that the lignum vitae tree, the wood of life, was the best tree for the job. It's found all around the Caribbean. Because of its toughness and heaviness, it's used for items such as mallets, ship pulleys, and the kind of batons often carried by policemen.

But I didn't know what the tree looked like. I was seven years old, and I remember going into the bush by myself carrying my dad's machete, looking for the right tree. Eventually, I went home and asked my dad to help me. He was the one who introduced me to the game, and I loved playing with him. I remember playing with his own cricket bat after a pickup game, doing what he loved. My dad helped me identify the small, purplish-blue flowers that adorned the tree, and its multicoloured, mottled bark. We chose the right tree and the right branch, cut it, and brought it home for him to carve.

Once we created my bat together, it never left my hand. It didn't matter where I was going, I carried it with me. My mom would listen for the noise of the cricket players, and she'd go there to find me. I was playing there seven days in the week. In my prayers, I wished that I had the power to make an eighth day so I'd have another extra day to play cricket.

Walking around with my cricket bat, I saw myself playing for the West Indies, but this didn't happen.

What did happen were some really good moments.

Moments with my dad, with my mom, with my big brother, who thought it was funny to see me walking around with that bat like it was a security blanket.

Moments with myself, dreaming about playing alongside Gary Sobers, even though he was twenty years older than me, and learning about how to see myself as a grown-up, taking part in something bigger than me.

Moments feeling like someone special carrying that bat, because I was academically behind at school at the time and dreaming made me feel big, like there was something ahead of me that I could look forward to achieving one day.

What I realized over time was that a dream is like a trunk of a tree that grows many branches. Not every branch bears fruit. But those branches that are not fruit-bearing, they do serve a purpose. Branches provide a shelter for some animals and food for others. They help us with the air we breathe. They can provide wood for a fire.

Dreams are the same way. There's no guarantee that you're going to realize your dreams. But you can use each one to fuel your ideas, your values, and your journey forward. When we start to dream about the life that we want, our dreams can provide us with the courage to imagine our future and who we want to be.

What is a dream?

Of course, you know what the two kinds of dreams are, at least superficially. There are the dreams you have at night when you are asleep, when your subconscious mind seems to play with things you know and things you do not. There are waking dreams in which we think about the many possible futures we have in front of us. In that way, both types of dreams are obviously alike in their ability to suggest new ideas to us, new pathways, new people, actions, and feelings.

The beautiful thing in either case is that dreams allow us to imagine something outside of the norm.

There is a group of people who live in northern Peru and eastern Ecuador called the Achuar who show us why this is the case.[1] Their cultural belief is that the dreams they have when they are sleeping are messages about their futures. The Achuar have an obligation to follow the instructions that they receive in their dreams. They believe that the dream state is one in which the human spirit leaves the physical world for a mythical one where discovering knowledge is easier. So, the state between sleep and waking is very important in their community.

The Achuar have three different types of dreams: the *kuntuknar*, the *mesekramprar*, and the *karamprar*.

Kuntuknar dreams tell the dreamer about a future success at work.

Mesekramprar dreams warn of a risk to the dreamer or their relations or close friends.

Karamprar dreams involve communication with other people, past or present.

In the community of the Achuar, dream interpretation is a constant presence. Families may awaken from dreams to interpret them on their own or with their loved ones, valuing the information to such a degree that they may choose not to share their dreams with people outside of their home. There are deeply defined rules for these interpretations that have been validated over generations. For the Achuar, a conscious thought process of reflecting and coding their dreams over a lifetime—a series of moments and snippets of information—can help them to reach their potential.

The Achuar might know something the rest of us don't.

Their way of life connects with what science has told us about conscious and subconscious dreaming. In fact, these kinds of dreams are actually more alike than we think when it comes to reaching our potential.

Why?

According to neuroscience, our brains operate in wave frequencies that help us to process knowledge and to learn.[2]

Our alpha state is when we are awake, aware, and relaxed. It's when the frequency of our brain waves oscillates between 8 and 12 hertz.

We may also move into a beta state if we become agitated or stressed out when we are awake. A beta state allows our minds and bodies to become more alert as we generate waves of up to 35 hertz.

When we are in a theta state, we're beginning to fall asleep or come out of it. This is when we have our most vivid dreams, when we are most deeply relaxed and our brains move to a slower pace of 4 to 8 hertz, characterized by uniquely long wave patterns.

Finally, when we move down to a hertz level of under 4, we're in a delta state, or deep sleep.

From a purely physical point of view, dreams take place when our minds reach a state of rest in which we are able to process information in a different way than when we are awake. Psychological research shows that what we see when we dream is likely to be a composite manifestation of many experiences that we have in real life and can point to what may need to be addressed, ultimately, in a conscious state. Our brain waves may alter from our conscious alpha or beta states to theta states when we dream, but the information that we have in our brains and our neural pathways does not change. In the theta stage, the human body deeply neutralizes stress. That's why a theta-wave dream state can perhaps help us to understand information that we have gathered through all of our senses, but for which we have no cognitive explanation.

Psychologists suggest that the dreams we have are indicators of what we may want to address in our waking lives but cannot. That's why so many of us want to find out what our dreams mean. Dreams can be important tools for self-awareness. The more we know and understand what our minds are processing, the more we may be able to reflect on what matters to us and what we may need to do in order to live in a more ideal waking state.

This is where the connection lies between our waking and sleeping dreams: there is an underlying human need for dreams for everyone, not just the Achuar. Dreaming allows us to present to our subconscious a problem that has the possibility of being solved. In this way, there is a deep connection between the process of dreaming and our ability to deal with difficult life challenges or imagining something new for ourselves.

Dreams, conscious and subconscious, give us purpose. Dreams ask us questions that we want to explore. They allow us to develop our challenging thoughts, turning them around and creating new ways of addressing what's bothering us, deep inside.

When I speak about dreams, I'm speaking about goals. I'm speaking about vision.

Your dreams can encompass anything you want, need, or desire.

But there is a caveat. Your dreams have to be *your* dreams. Not someone else's.

Let's look at New Year's resolutions, for example. These are simple dreams that most of us come up with every year. According to a recent study, if you have a single New Year's resolution, your likelihood of failure is said to be about 80 percent.[3] If you dream up a number of different resolutions, however, you might actually be successful at all of them.

Dreams, conscious and subconscious, give us purpose.

Why is that? Psychologically, when we pressurize ourselves into achieving one goal, we can feel an overwhelming fear of our own success. We also focus on what we think we must do in life, like shedding weight or finishing a degree, rather than on exploring what we want to do with our free time. When we open ourselves up to a number of dreams, we are on a mission of discovery to see what we might do.

The dreams that you call into being can bring you fulfillment and joy on a level that you haven't experienced before, but they have to be your unique dreams. And you are not only allowed to but *should* chase the *biggest* dreams you want to chase. Your dream tree can grow and develop, providing you with light and shade, according to how you decide to tend it.

How do we figure out how to identify our dreams?

How can we make decisions about building a life of passion that can bear fruit?

In my case, I let my dreams guide me forward. As a kid, I knew I loved playing sports. After I immigrated to Canada with my family, I still wanted to be Gary Sobers, but I also wanted to be Ken Dryden. Soon, the basketball Hall of Famer Kareem Abdul-Jabbar won the NBA championship in Milwaukee and, as a tall kid, I started to look up to him as well. By the time I was in university, I was spending my Saturdays running basketball clinics because I really enjoyed the game.

What I didn't know was that I would love working with children so much. While teaching basketball, I found it so easy to connect with them and it was so easy for them to connect with me. There was something special happening, right there on the court.

I wanted to bounce.

I realized that I was bouncing when I was around the children. It seemed like I was going higher and higher. I realized that I liked the idea of working with children more than I wanted to play basketball on my own. My dream wasn't created, it was revealed through trial and error. I learned what worked for me and what didn't work by just participating in one of my dream sports, and the dream automatically adjusted.

Looking at those children and their smiling faces, I had no choice but to see the branches that were actually bearing fruit on my dream tree. That's when I made the decision to become an educator. We all need something to give us some bounce, and there it was, seeing those kids' faces light up when I planted that seed of excitement for them.

But if it wasn't for that initial dream of being a sportsman, I wouldn't have planted my own seed. I wouldn't have watched it grow into a dream tree. I wouldn't have seen its branches spread out and upwards.

When you're planting a seed, be confident that it will grow. Most seeds, either literal or figurative, find a way to if their minimum care requirements are met. Many seeds are hardy; for example, a kale plant will grow even in colder weather. Of course, you want your seed to grow. It will grow as big as you want it to be. But that doesn't mean the tree will look exactly like you imagined it to be.

Dreams develop your skills and introduce you to new ones.

Dreams change you so that you see new possibilities.

Dreams open you up to meeting new people.

And what happens then? You're going to end up having a dream or goal or desire that will end up growing branches, because that's what dreams do. You're going to feel that your dream is valid when you get that clear message.

And the message will be clear.

Start imagining your dream tree into being.

Everyone was born with the potential to fulfill their biggest and most intangible dream, and I mean every one of the approximately eight billion people on earth. No one came into our world without it. Dreaming is our gift at birth and dreaming becomes the gift to our community, country, and ourselves when we are working to realize it.

I believe that I am living my own dream, because I spend a lot of time in the middle of my own Venn diagram. I have lived a life working with adults and children in three worlds—teaching, parenting, and coaching. I believe that the essence of these three vocations is helping those in my care to grow a positive mindset and reach their potential.

Here's where we start raising your roof with practical exercises. Take your time with these exercises! They are tried and tested ways to get you to start exploring, making intentions to seed your potential, and planning your dream goals.

Exercise Your Potential: Your Dream Venn

I want you to fill in your own Venn diagram.

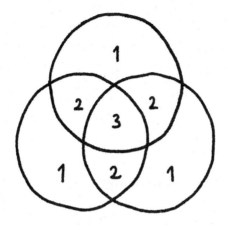

1. What are the three things you like doing the most in life? Write each one down in one of the outer circles labelled 1.
2. Now, draw connections between each set of two activities. Where do these two overlap? What actions are similar between them? Write them down in the overlapping triangles labelled 2.
3. Finally, what's the same about all three of these activities? Write that down in the inner triangle labelled 3.

In the Venn diagram, what connects your worlds is important. For me, doing this exercise helped me define my mission in life: it demonstrated for me the actions from which I derive the most meaning. Living in my personal Venn diagram means that what I enjoy most is standing up in front of teachers, students, and leaders, telling them inspirational stories about people who have achieved their dreams in spite of the odds. The connecting point for me is the word *potential*.

Now, I'm going to ask you some questions that I want you to think about in detail when you have a spare moment to reflect. These questions will continue to arise throughout the book. You can use a journal to answer these questions, and you can also think about them when you are taking a walk or getting ready for your day.

If you want a valuable trick for reflection, record yourself speaking your dreams, beliefs, and actions out loud. Use your phone as a recorder, or you can even use a transcription app so you can easily review your ideas after each session.

Here goes.

Dreaming: Connection Points

What is your *real* connecting point to your potential? Not an idea or action that you think you have to do, but the one that you actually want to do. Think about that connecting point further. How does that idea or action link to the biggest dream you can imagine for yourself? Remember, it can be anything.

You'll hone your connecting point and your dream as we move through this book, but take a look inside yourself and think about what you might actually want to *do* every day.

How do you want to feel every day?

What does that dream look like for you?

Write it down or record it electronically.

Now, think about the other parts of your own three-legged stool. Dreaming is not enough, and, in fact, we are only given the pieces to build our stool. We have to create it on our own. No one came into the world with a stool that is completed. In fact, think about whether anyone has ever removed the chair you were about to sit on, literally or figuratively. The one thing that your parents, teachers, doctors, or coaches can't do is to reach your potential for you. You must take ownership of it and do the work to put your stool together. No one can do that work for you.

But as writer Gretchen Rubin tells us, just because we're busy doesn't mean we're being productive. Working is one of the most dangerous forms of procrastination.[4]

We can't just work *around* our goals, we have to work *towards* them. We can't just look busy, we have to take our dreams seriously. Each of us has to put time into dreaming, believing, and doing that work. It is said that Rome was not built in a day. The famous adage makes the point that great things take time to accomplish. There is greatness in you and me, but is not an overnight thing.

Your potential will not be reached in a day. Your stool will not be built in a day. You won't be believing and doing everything just yet. And that's okay.

As you turn the pages of this book, think about what you'd like your own story to look like. If I were going to stand up and use your life story to inspire the next generation of students, what story would you want me to tell the children in the auditorium?

Think about your dreams and how they relate to the life story that you want to share with others. Think about how your dream life can inform the choices that you are making today.

Believe in what you might be able to accomplish if you set your mind on your dream path.

Start to consider just what you'll have to do to get there.

And one final note: While you're imagining your dreams, speak to yourself softly. Remember that you are the author of the conversation playing out in your mind. The world is lining up to take shots at you; don't take them at yourself.

Tell yourself what is good for your mind to hear, and acknowledge that flame burning deep within you.

CHAPTER 5

Unlabel Yourself

They used to call me Billy Dee back at Cordella Junior Public School. It was my first professional teaching assignment.

It was a compliment back in the early 1980s to evoke the actor who played the great Lando Calrissian in the original *Star Wars* film series. Billy Dee Williams was known for his moustache and his swagger and his smile. He was one cool dude, and I felt lucky to be compared to him.

But, unlike Lando, I wasn't running Cloud City. I was working hard in one of the most challenging inner-city schools in Toronto. And I wasn't having the easiest time when I first got started because I had inherited a class after the previous teacher was fired. It wasn't really clear what had happened. I knew that the school was known to be tough, but I couldn't imagine what a teacher would have to do to be removed from a position where demand for educators outstripped local supply. Because it was the class nobody wanted to teach, the school had called me up right out of university. I wanted to get my foot in the door, so I accepted the challenge without a second thought.

My first day, I met the teacher in the classroom next to mine.

"Karl, if they assigned those kids to me," she said, hands on her hips and shaking her head, "I would leave this school. Are you sure you know what you're doing?"

"No, Cheryl. I don't. But I'll take them. I got this."

I started with a unit on Australia. Surprisingly, there was a play at the Young People's Theatre on that very subject. So in the next teaching staff meeting, I announced that I would be taking my kids to the theatre.

"Karl, you're making a mistake. It's going to be chaos," I heard across the table. "And you're the one who's going to get the brunt of it. We don't allow these kids to leave the building."

"These children are not a mistake," I said, my passion evident to those around me. "So as long as I have your permission to try this out, it's going to be just fine."

At the time I started teaching there, all of the children at Cordella were labelled high-risk. But I don't get caught up with labels. Because I've lived my life in the field of education, I don't see any child through the lens of a label. Who knows what they're capable of doing with the potential that's inside of them? No one knows. But instead of seeing children through this enormous potential that they have, sometimes we see them through only the lens of their most challenging demographics or their cognitive development, or, God forbid, their tiny, childlike failures. We're limiting them when we do that.

I told the kids we were going to see a show, and I was excited.

"I want you to put on your Sunday best. I want you to get ready. This is going to be a great learning experience."

When we arrived at the Young People's Theatre, we were surrounded by children from private schools in their uniforms and jackets. They were clambering over seats, running, screaming, these privileged kids in their colour-coded outfits. They had the run of the place. They had been to the theatre many times in their lives. My kids knew they were lucky to be there, out of school for a few hours to experience something new and different.

My kids were the best-behaved group of kids there. Because I believed in them and I saw their potential, I knew that the bar I set for them would be the bar they achieved.

When I returned to the school, I decided to set the bar higher for everyone. There was paper all over the place, garbage. One morning, after the janitors had made their usual rounds and cleaned the place spotless, I decided to add some welcome signs and plants in the foyer.

"Mr. Subban, don't buy plants," I was told. "The kids are going to destroy them."

Guess what? The plants are still there today.

That first year, my own name changed. I was no longer Billy Dee. Instead, I was Cordella's number-one teacher. They gave me a medallion with that slogan printed right on it.

All I did was recognize that how we see others influences how they see themselves, and that includes our children. Too often, we prepare the path for the child instead the child for the path.

We adults don't see ourselves clearly, either. Often, we set the bar for ourselves too low. Way too low.

Just like with children labelled high-risk, our own problems begin when we start to connect with each other and to our own self-image through a label.

Where do we get these labels? And why do they stick to us?

We hear them every day, especially when we're kids.

At school, even as early as kindergarten, we get labelled as autistic, as having ADHD or a learning disability or poor eyesight. In some ways, that's a blessing because when we know what's getting in the way of our learning, we can use really useful, tried-and-true methods to get going on the path to our education. But even so, the labels still stick beyond their usefulness. As well as learning how to read and write, we learn that we've been put into one kind of box or another.

At home, we also get labelled by our parents and siblings. We're the funny one, the smart one, the pretty one. Sometimes we're even labelled as the lazy one, the one who won't do as they are told, or the disappointment. And, as a result, we either keep up appearances and remain in one of those boxes, or we try to fight our way out of them.

Often, we set the bar for ourselves too low. Way too low.

When we get to university or start work, we also get labelled once again. We have to learn to market ourselves to the world, and so we look for the labels that we think others want to see and slap those on our chests. We make a list of those labels and call it a résumé.

What's the problem with labels, you say? Sounds like they can help, at least for the most part. Labels get us access to resources. They allow us to get a job in our field. Sure, that's all true.

But a label is also a kind of roof. It puts us in a box, and that box is usually closed. We don't want to have labels, especially because they are so sticky.

We're unique human beings.

We come into the world unlabelled.

We don't need to be stuck.

But remember, as always, even if someone has given us a label, there are many things we can change about ourselves. We don't want to place a roof over our heads, but we also can't let others constrain how we define who we are, either.

Exercise Your Potential: Label-Maker

Let's think about the labels we're given, and the ones we give ourselves, good and bad.

The author Stephen Covey designed a great analogy in his book *The 7 Habits of Highly Effective People*.[1] We each have a wide range of concerns, from health to family, from problems at work to whether a foreign leader is about to start a nuclear war. Within what Covey calls the Circle of Concern are the things over which we have no control. Reactive people tend to focus their efforts on the Circle of Concern, which can result in blaming, accusing attitudes and the ever-increasing feeling that the world is happening only to them. Proactive people prefer to focus their efforts on a different circle, the Circle of Influence, working on those things they can actually do something about. This positive energy causes their Circle of Influence to expand.

So, the basic thing that Covey is communicating is that there are some parts of our lived experience that we can control: those things that stand within our Circle of Influence. But there are a lot more things we can't control: the events and factors in our Circle of Concern. Sure, we're going to be concerned about our Circle of Concern; that's literally what it's all about. But highly proactive people, Covey suggests, recognize their "Response-ability"—the ability to choose how they will respond to a given stimulus or situation.

Take an onion. Each onion has a core that is covered by layers upon layers that are created as it grows. We are the same. Each and every one of us has a unique core at our centre. However, during our lives, we accumulate layers like those of the onion to both protect us and to cover up our unique self. Layers emerge from the various interactions we experience in life. We may add layers when we are vulnerable, when we are hurt by a dear friend, or when we were punished after acting out in a way that our parents didn't approve of.

Each layer provides us with a buffer between who we really are and the world around us.

This pattern continues to the point where we have so many layers, we don't remember who we are anymore. At some point, we disconnect from our own selves, from our own core.

If we look at our labels using a similar analogy, we might come up with a circle that looks a little bit like this:

Think carefully about this model before you start to fill in your own circle.

Start on the outside.

How does the world see you without knowing anything about you? What label would a stranger slap on you at first glance? Write those words or phrases down.

For example, a stranger looking at me might use these labels: male, tall, Black, smiling, confident, open to conversation (and not necessarily in that order). They might see me wearing a hockey team jacket and assume I have something to do with the sport, whether I'm a fan, a coach, or a dad. Many people would label me as Jamaican, because they can hear my slight accent.

Now move inward.

How do people you know label you?

My sons might label me a father; other people might name me as their coach or their teacher. A lot of people will label me as a relentlessly positive person, a dog with a bone talking about raising that roof. Still others would say that I give the best hugs of anyone they know. But there are people who might see the worst in me, too. I've been told I talk about hockey too much. I've been told I laugh too easily and spread my time too thin.

Finally, get into that inner circle.

What labels do you put on yourself? What do you honestly think about who you are?

When I think about myself, I call myself a coach. That has always been the essence of who I am, from a very young age. I also label myself as respectful. I treat others in a way that tells them that they have value. I see myself as a good friend, a good parent, and a good grandparent. I love spending time with people I love.

As you start to write things down, really get to the bottom of how you are labelling yourself. If you start to think about yourself as stupid, lazy, or unworthy, think hard about whether that is a "my labels for me" or whether that word should move into an outer circle. Is it something your parent or sibling said to you? Then it doesn't belong in the inner circle; it belongs in "others' labels for me." Is it a word attached to how the world feels about your race, religion, culture, or language? Then it doesn't belong in the inner circle; it belongs in "the world's labels for me."

It's okay to put the burden of a label onto someone else, even your own family members. Some people are like nails: they know how to deflate your tires. Others pump you up. But you're not them and they're not you. Are you a nail or a pump? Put the responsibility for your labels where they genuinely belong.

Keep moving those labels into the right places until the labels in the centre circle are only what you authentically feel about who you are right now.

Now, look at that centre circle and decide if those labels represent the person you want to be. What labels do you want to add? Subtract? Can you ask yourself why you are labelling yourself in the way that you do?

Add in some new labels, ones that define the you you want to be.

You need to have what I call Potential Awareness in order to raise your roof. It's exactly what it sounds like. There really is nothing standing in your way of doing something amazing and being the person you want to be. The labels you know yourself by aren't really real, but they are beams in your roof. When you understand and believe that you can learn, grow, and develop, even with those labels others are trying to stick on you, you have the awareness to shrug them off.

Other people's labels are about them, not about you.

We all encounter hardships and obstacles. Sometimes labels reinforce the roof over our potential. To clear the roof, you have to clear the labels, too.

On June 23, 1940, a premature baby girl, Wilma, was born to Blanche and Ed Rudolph in Tennessee. Her early birth left her health unstable, and as a child, Wilma suffered from double pneumonia and scarlet fever. At four, she contracted polio and suffered from infantile paralysis. She had to wear a brace on her left leg. But Wilma didn't let that stop her. With the help of physical therapy and personal determination, she was able to walk. At the age of eleven, she started playing basketball at Cobb Elementary School in Clarksville. Later, at Tennessee State University, Wilma began training seriously and won a bronze medal in the 400-metre relay in the 1956 Olympic Games. At the next Olympic Games in 1960,

Wilma won three golds in track, the first American woman to do so in a single Olympics. When she was celebrated back home in Tennessee, she adamantly insisted that her homecoming parade, which thousands lined the city streets to watch, was fully integrated during the Jim Crow–era southern United States.

The world around her at the time of her birth would have labelled Wilma as Black, disabled, female, and, essentially, without a great deal of value. Blanche and Ed labelled her their daughter, and they believed in her fully, giving her all of the love she needed. Wilma labelled herself an Olympic gold medalist and activist, and, later, an educator.

There are three types of people when it comes down to Potential Awareness.

First, there are those who see the roof, but it's permanent. It's made of solid beams, rafters, and decking that are impossible to dislodge. They have no idea why they're stuck. In fact, some people are harder on themselves than a hammer hitting them.

Then, there is the second group of people, those who see the roof and know that it's going to take a lot of hard work and expense to open it up. They're not sure if they can muster the energy to raise that roof, but they always have the intention to move those beams above their heads. They weigh the pros and cons endlessly and might take a few steps forward and a few back.

The third type of person says, "I don't see a roof, because nothing's gonna stop me." This can be a good thing. Coming from a certain type of person, however, it might also be a sign of delusion! But believing in the possibility of raising your roof is a pathway to loving and accepting yourself, embracing what you want, and letting all the happiness into your life.

Most of us are probably in the second group, and that's okay. But unfortunately, intentions are not enough.

Dreaming: Potential Awareness

When it comes down to Potential Awareness, what type of person are you right now?

Reflect on how you are going to grow into your potential if you don't have the level of Potential Awareness that you feel you need.

Have you noticed that some of the changes you make in your life are often only short-term fixes? Why do you think that is the case?

Regardless of how you modify your life, does a lack of Potential Awareness sometimes creep back in?

Remember, we're all born with potential and it takes Potential Awareness to realize it. Sometimes the labels we've been handed end up covering up that awareness.

We have to move our labels back to where they belong.

And we need to see ourselves as dynamite.

We can blow away our roof without any fear that we aren't worthy.

CHAPTER 6

Define Your Own Needs

In the summer of 1938, when he was thirty years old, American psychologist Abraham Maslow spent six weeks living at the Siksika Reserve, the home of one of the four Indigenous Niitsítapi nations of the Blackfoot Confederacy. It's about an hour's drive east of Calgary, Alberta, in the plains north of the Bow River.

Maslow arrived at Siksika with two of his colleagues from the University of Wisconsin: anthropologists Jane Richardson Hanks and Lucien Hanks. The reason he visited was that Jane and Lucien suggested that Maslow could learn from the Blackfoot. Maslow was studying what he called "social dominance," namely that the way in which people interact with one another is based on the individual power they hold.

Except that there was a problem. What he learned about Blackfoot culture didn't have anything to do with what most people think about social power.

Maslow was used to top-down power systems, just like most of us in the Western world. We're used to looking up to kings, queens, presidents, prime ministers, celebrities, and business moguls. We automatically think that people who have individual power deserve it in some way.

The Blackfoot people that Maslow met on his journey, however, didn't think like that.

Like many Indigenous peoples, their wealth itself was no prize; it was their ability to give to others that brought prestige in their community. The more they acquired, the more they were able to give away. This brought stability and happiness to the people in their settlements.

Watching them interact with each other, as well, offered a sharp contrast to the racism and conflict he saw arising from the settlers who lived in close proximity to the reserve. As Maslow wrote to a friend at the time, "The more I got to know the whites in the village, who were the worst bunch of creeps and bastards I'd ever run across in my life, the more it got paradoxical."[1] The paradox, he wrote, was that he had gone to Alberta with the assumption that he, a white man, knew better and that the Blackfoot were a more primitive society. It was only when he lived among them that he recognized that the opposite might be the truth.

When Maslow got back home, he wrote about his experience with the Blackfoot, trying to piece together what made their society seem so elegant and supportive. As a social psychologist, he wanted to understand what worked so that he could make recommendations about how people could live their lives in a way that would make them happier and more fulfilled.

In 1943, Maslow turned his experience with the Blackfoot into his most well-known theory, the hierarchy of needs.[2] Maslow created a model in which the absolute pinnacle of human experience is reached when we get to a place in which all of our needs are finally met.

You've heard of this model, I am sure.

At the bottom of the pyramid of needs are fundamental things like our physiological and safety needs. We have to have our basic needs like food, a home, and foundational security in place if we want to do anything else with our lives. Otherwise, we'll only be motivated to find food and shelter. In his model, Maslow made the argument that, once those needs are met, a person can move towards meeting their love and belonging needs, esteem needs, and finally their self-actualization needs. Self-actualization is when we feel fulfilled by our work and our life, and we do not feel a sense of longing for something we have not yet achieved. At this point in our lives, we have met our potential.

But, in fact, for the Blackfoot, that pyramid was reversed.[3]

> To support yourself, you have to be your own mentor, and that starts with defining your values in your own hierarchy of needs.

Dr. Cindy Blackstock from McGill University, also a member of the Gitxsan Nation, suggests that self-actualization is actually at the bottom of the pyramid.

Her interpretation of the hierarchy of needs, compared to Maslow's, looks something like this:

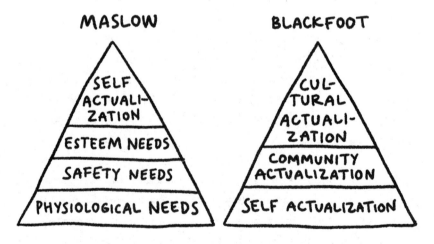

The Blackfoot concept of niita'pitapi, someone who is completely developed or who has arrived, is a person who has high levels of both empathy and self-esteem and who has an outstanding quality of life. This self-actualization had to precede community actualization and the accumulation of collective, rather than personal, wealth.

But instead of asking the question of how individuals could become niita'pitapi, the Blackfoot helped their children to see their self-worth early in life. Blackfoot children were taught that they arrived on earth already worthy, good, and valuable, and that they had nothing to prove to others. This point of view allowed them to feel safe and secure. It created a community in which helping others, building their culture, and supporting everyone's quality of life was expected.

Why are we on this journey to reach our potential?

To be better than our neighbours?

To check off all of the boxes of life?

To make it to the highest level of the game we're playing?

No. We are on this journey to reach our potential to feel satisfied in who we are. We are on this journey to feel emotionally, physically, and intellectually ourselves.

What if reaching our potential results from building human connection, consciousness, and curiosity?

What if we didn't have to try so hard?

What if we didn't have to hold ourselves to the habits of billionaires, supermodels, and athletes we watch or read about in lifestyle posts?

A few years ago, I took a flight and ended up sitting beside a nice young woman who had grown up in London, Ontario. Soon enough, we started talking about personal growth. When I least expected it, she started to cry. She told me about herself, and she was so accomplished. She was running a business in Sweden. But then, she broke down as she shared the details.

In school, she felt like she had to get straight As.

She went to the business school she thought she had to attend.

She got married because it was expected of her.

Now, her parents wanted her to have a child.

But she wanted to have a life.

I remember her saying that all the choices she'd made in her life, she made them for other people. She was reaching for the top of the pyramid. She wanted to be the best of the best, and it wasn't making her happy.

"At least now you are aware of what's causing your discomfort," I said to her. "Now, you have the ability to do something about it."

If you try to be all things to all people, you will end up being nothing to no one.

If you want to reach your potential, you have to start being honest with yourself.

We live in a constant state of survival and urgency. There's a difference between surviving and thriving. Many of us spend most of our days just in survival mode. "If I can just get through the morning," we say to ourselves. "If I can just get through the meeting, if I can just get through the week . . ." We do this because we feel like that's the only way we're going to get through that ceiling and start thriving.

But whether you follow Abraham Maslow's way of thinking or that of the Blackfoot, the outcome isn't good if you're constantly on edge. To support yourself, you have to be your own mentor, and that starts with defining your values in your own hierarchy of needs.

Sheila Johnson was the first Black female billionaire in the United States. She co-founded the incredibly successful Black Entertainment Television, which she recently sold for $3 billion. She's also an owner in three professional sports franchises: the

Washington Capitals (NHL), the Washington Wizards (NBA), and the Washington Mystics (WNBA).

As Johnson writes, there is no such thing as overnight success. You need three things to reach your potential: the right plan, the right timing, and the right people alongside you.[4] If you're going to achieve your goals, Johnson explains, you have to keep your head in the game and define your values. Why? Because every single person who takes a risk is going to walk through fire. That's the reason that Johnson named her newest company Salamander Hotels and Resorts, of which she is CEO. She learned that, in Greek mythology, the salamander is the only creature that can walk through fire and come out the other end alive. Keeping yourself in the game at all times and not letting outside influences get to you means that *you* define who you are, what you want to achieve, and how you're going to do it.

For me, I value hard work, perseverance, dedication to my community, keeping my word, and integrity in everything I try to do.

I value honesty.

I value trust.

When I work with young people, I'm all in; it is a deep-rooted passion of mine, and that's not going to change. But, like many educators and coaches, when it comes to trying to reach my own potential, I will often work harder for others than I do for myself. I think it has something to do with how we're socialized, whether it's cultural or just personal. Even if you value honesty and integrity and hard work, if you are socialized to believe that other people go first, your time can be spent supporting others rather than your own goals.

It's not that we want to get rid of all of our societal values. Of course, we want to recognize that social pressures exist and that some of these pressures, like parents encouraging their children to get an education, come from a place of wanting the best for each other. But, like the example of the woman I met on the plane, social pressures sometimes stop us from reaching our potential. Those values that we were socialized to adopt are like old recordings, playing over and over again in our heads.

Each of us have our own values, ones we've built a lifetime working towards. We also see value statements on websites and in offices. This, our values, is our mission, this is what is important to us. The problem with values is that sometimes we only value the good outcomes—innovation, respect, honour. We don't value being told we're wrong. We don't value learning. We don't value putting in the work. We don't value the behaviours that lead to personal growth because we haven't done the hard work of self-awareness, other-awareness, and intention building. We don't value the real changes we need to make because we were off course in the first place. We hate being wrong. If a company says that they value constant improvement, for example, they may not value the hard conversations it actually takes to get to true, sustained improvement.

Everyone thrives in their own unique way. The woman I met on the plane learned that if she didn't focus on her own unique needs, then she wouldn't feel successful or take on the roles she actually wanted. This became her defining moment. Thinking about the role she wanted was how she began to take a hard look at all her opportunities, how she scheduled her time, and how she could prioritize the obligations she had to herself.

In that moment of realization, she began to take care of her priority role: herself.

Freedom from fear allows us to move into choosing. Really choosing.

Think about a person who chooses what they might think of as a "righteous path," namely one that has been defined by society as being not only acceptable, but preferred. The path of the righteous person is narrow, however. It is the choice to, for example, go to law school because your parents think it's the right thing to do, even though you want to be a dancer and every fibre of your being is calling you to make dance your priority. It is actually the path of least resistance because it is following what others want for us, where we can never be criticized and where we will get the most support. If you go to law school, your parents might provide you with money to take your degree, but if you become a dancer, you may be on your own even though it is the less lucrative path.

Fearing the unknown, therefore, means that deep and socially supported myths and pervasive statements follow us everywhere. Often there are nuggets of wisdom in there, too, such as the reality that lawyers make more money than dancers, which could matter to some individuals. But we often choose the path of least resistance for different reasons, emotional reasons. And these emotional reasons are often grounded in fear: fear of being socially isolated, fear of being cut off from economic support, fear of the unknown path. When we get even deeper, we realize that this is a fear of ourselves. Fear of not being safe or worthy or enough.

You can follow your fear until you can't hold out any longer, or you can follow your courage and meet with intention whatever it is you happen to meet. In this way, fear and courage are similar to context and identity.

People can actually do amazing things when they are very frightened. Is that courage, then? When given no choice, it is easy to choose. If I run through this burning room, I *might* die, but if I stay in this burning house, I will die *for sure*! So is that courage or desperate self-preservation?

Exercise Your Potential: Your Needs, Your Hierarchy

Take a minute and create your own hierarchy of needs. What are the fundamental values at the base of your pyramid that should always be a part of your everyday life? What is optional? What is at the top of your pyramid? What is your ultimate values-based goal in life?

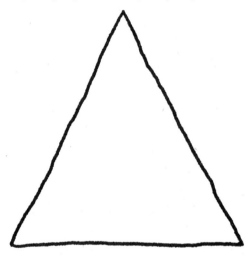

YOUR VALUES-BASED NEEDS

Now, think about your current life roles and how you invest your current time. Make a list of all the roles that you have: worker, parent, caretaker, cook, cleaner, community organizer, volunteer, anything you see yourself doing on a regular basis. These roles can be official or unofficial. They can be paid or unpaid, they can be easy or difficult.

Dreaming: What's Your Level?

Have you given up any of your values over the course of your lifetime?

How can you make sure that your own values don't get superseded by the values that were placed on you?

How can you know and decide what values really ought to matter in your life?

What are ways that you can thrive while maintaining your values?

How can you let yourself shine through the social noise?

What do you spend your time doing?

Are your current roles in life putting you in survival mode or do they allow you to thrive?

How do you feel in these roles?

If you don't see what you want to see in your roles, ask yourself if what you are doing every day matches up with your pyramid?

What are you missing in terms of being honest with yourself right now? Are you like the woman on the plane, investing time in the things that others expect from you? Or are you investing in yourself?

Now think of the roles that you feel like you thrive in. What do you see yourself doing?

Courage is choosing, when we have a choice.

What we all need in the hierarchy of our lives is to set ourselves up as a priority.

We need to invest our time and energy in the things that matter to us, otherwise we won't be able to reach our potential. We ought to be able to spend our time and effort building the kind of life that we love.

When we strive to embrace this perspective and work on loving ourselves now, what exactly are we loving? The pretend version of ourselves, or something else?

It is only by becoming our own priority that we can be healthy, safe, and able to move towards our potential. As we begin to take care of ourselves, we can schedule and commit time to what we love. We might do that by spending time alone, by journalling, by feeding our needs so that we feel at ease and able to do the harder tasks we have in front of us.

With greater awareness comes greater responsibility, almost un-limited potential, and perhaps the recognition of our true superpower.

When the curtain is drawn back on who we are and the difference between ourselves and our pretend selves is revealed, then the work really begins.

CHAPTER 7

Become a Dream Leader

My good friend Sam was working in a department that he loved, and he brought a lot of value to his team. He worked long hours, often from eight in the morning till eight at night. He was a true company man, as they used to call him.

One day, Sam's supervisor, Michael, told him that he was eventually going to be moving back to his home country of Ireland.

"When I'm ready to make that move, I'm going to tell the owner of the company that you should get my job," he said. "You need to be in a leadership position. You've proven to us that you can do it, and I'm not going to leave until they've confirmed that you're going to be my replacement."

Sam was thrilled, as any of us would be. The day came when Michael left, after he wrote a long letter of recommendation about Sam to the owner of the company. One of Sam's co-workers came up to him and asked him a question.

"Sam, did you meet the new supervisor? I just ran into him in the hallway. I thought Michael was making you our new boss, wasn't he?"

"What do you mean?" Sam asked, aghast. "They hired someone new?"

Sam was livid. He went in to see the owner of the company.

"I just heard that you hired someone to take over the leadership of my department," he said. "I had been promised that job. I saw the letter Michael delivered last week. What happened?"

The owner of the company started hemming and hawing, looking down at his desk, not meeting Sam in the eye. Sam could see that the man was not going to relent, but more than that, his boss didn't have any integrity. Sam noticed a notepad on the corner of the desk. Sam has really good penmanship, and he started writing something on the pad, and, when he was finished, he handed it to his boss.

"That's my two weeks' notice. I'm going to work my last two weeks as if I was going to stay here for another fifty years, because I keep my commitments," he said.

Sam then turned, walked out, and returned to his department. He didn't have another job lined up, but he knew he needed to be treated better than that. Even so, he did his job consistently and accurately until the day he left. Even under adversity, Sam stood up for his values, not knowing where his next steps would take him. His words matched his actions. He knew that he was a really good employee, that he was dedicated. He was committed. He also didn't want to collect a paycheque from someone he couldn't trust.

It was less than a week after giving his notice when Sam's brother told him about an opportunity to buy a small business, but Sam worked his two weeks, not leaving a minute earlier than he had promised.

Unsurprisingly, it didn't take long for Sam and his brother to become successful business owners. Within a short period of time, the growing and successful business was making a profit. They still run the business today.

Sam was evolving as a person, towards his own potential and towards his own version of leadership. Because he lived through the impact of top-down decision-making, he went on to be the kind of employer who values his team members and their own unique contributions. He moved away from acting based on others' decisions towards acting as an expert in his own life and trusting others to become experts in theirs.

Even more important, Sam made it a priority to follow his dream rather than simply play out a role for someone else at a company in which he had no stake. There was a clear parallel between Sam's readiness to lead and his ability to reach his potential. His confidence to make the move to working for himself was intrinsically connected to his personal growth. Sam didn't only have commitment and clarity, but also the integrity to see his plans through to success.

Likewise, the most important person to lead you to your potential is you. Who better to be an expert on you than *you*?

I'd like you to take a moment and truly think about what leadership means to you.

What does leadership look like in your life experiences?

What does it look like when you picture yourself as a leader?

When you think of leadership and of yourself taking on a leadership role, do the same images emerge?

Or do you think of the leadership approaches of other people as separate from the way that you envision your own leadership potential?

Dreaming: Leadership

Leadership and dreaming are linked.

I remember standing in the schoolyard on the first day of classes at Claireville Junior School. We had a routine where all the staff would come out and meet the students and their families. As the principal, the goal I set was for all the educators to be visible. Visible leaders make a difference; invisible leaders do not. And as a leader of a school, it's important to be visible to all the stakeholders, the parents, the students, and everyone in the community at large.

That day, beyond the yard, I could see a Black mother and her small child on the sidewalk just a short distance from me. The child's face was full of uncertainty. I was thinking to myself about how the first day of school is a time of transitioning from summertime back to the classroom, not an easy thing for any child. Behind me, I could hear the school bell ring out. I looked back, and I saw the other children moving inside with their assigned teachers, but there was little Madison, still hugging her mother like a snake wrapped around a tree. She was holding on and wouldn't let go.

I said to myself, "Okay, I better move in and help."

That's when I became the tree. Madison's mom handed her off to me, and she took to my shoulder.

"She's just going into kindergarten," Madison's mom said. "She's a little scared."

"It's okay," I said. "I'd be a little scared if I were in her position. She's a green strawberry, not quite ready. Leave her with me."

I brought her inside to my office and put her down to give her a little bit more freedom, and we got to talking. I sat with Madison and then gave her some paper to draw on while I shuffled my own papers. It was long enough to help her shift the way she was feeling and get her calm enough to take some new steps forward.

"I want you to promise me something, Madison."

"Okay," she said hesitantly.

"Listen, you've been here for about an hour. That's great. It was so nice for you to spend this time with Mr. Subban, because we got to know each other, and that is so important. Now I'm gonna walk you down to your classroom. And I'll tell you what, when recess comes, I'm gonna meet you outside. Is that okay?"

"That is okay." She nodded.

Madison went calmly to her classroom, and when the bell rang for recess less than an hour later, I made myself visible again. She came out to walk around with me, barely as tall as my knee.

But for every recess for many days, for many weeks into the school year, Madison kept showing up to find me again. She was my shadow. She didn't say much, but she was always there with me.

One day, she tapped me on the knee.

"Mr. Subban, I'd like to ask you a question."

When a child asks me a question, I bend down on one knee so that they can see my face.

"Mr. Subban, did the cow really jump over the moon?" Madison whispered in her kindergarten voice.

I tried not to laugh. She must have heard that "Hey, diddle, diddle" Mother Goose nursery rhyme in class. But with kids, however much you want to encourage their sense of play, you also have to be honest with them.

"No," I said. "The cow didn't jump over the moon. But you can reach for the moon. You know, reaching for the moon, you might just touch some stars."

I remembered, in that moment, why I was there, why I was a principal. I wanted to remind every child I knew that, in life, we can all reach for something. In showing Madison that I cared and that I was there for her, I opened up a dialogue. For her to want to ask me that question, she had to know that I believed in her ability to dream. When she closed her eyes, Madison didn't have to imagine a cow jumping over the moon. She could imagine absolutely anything at all.

Being a leader means that you do things for the right reason so that people have a reason to follow you. Madison followed me around the school because I gave her a reason to trust me. I let her be herself, on her own schedule. Together, we created a dream for her to excel at school.

Dreams provide a pathway to the unknown, untapped potential that we all possess.

Dreams create worlds.

Awake or asleep, dreams allow us to travel to places where there are more possibilities.

Dreams are imaginary, expanding states of consciousness that tell our own story and make the world what we want it to be.

It is important for us to dream. We have to believe that what we desire is infinitely possible.

But we must also empower ourselves to turn our thoughts towards leadership if we want to create dreams that embody our potential.

To do this, we can't overrate other people's abilities and, in doing so, underestimate our own ability to lead. In fact, each of us has to learn to lead if we want to learn how to live. That's because without leadership, we have no sense of direction and we're not going to get too far along the path towards our dreams.

And our leadership abilities are connected to the meaning we take from our dreams.

Have the people who've stopped chasing their dreams reached success or happiness?

Do they find their dreams unattainable? Perhaps.

Are they afraid of feeling successful? Maybe.

Reaching our potential comes from contentment. It's the feeling that something has been achieved, been underlined. It's the point at which we can relax. Reaching our potential is like the feeling of finally exhaling after holding our breath for a very long time.

But part of the problem with actually accepting our own dreams is that the world we live in is so full of information and the rules of life are being rewritten every moment of the day. Even though we each have the ability to dream about any goal we want to set for ourselves, we sometimes forget that we are the only people who can make that dream happen. That's why we have to see ourselves as leaders in our own lives, rather than rely on someone else to facilitate our dreams for us.

Every time we give hope, time, and effort to a dream, we can start to see the world from a new perspective. When we want to raise our roof, the only thing we have to remember is that we won't get it wrong if we focus on our dreams first.

That doesn't mean there isn't more work to be done. But the way that we do it is likely to look very different in the future if we allow for two things:

1. There is always an authentic possibility that our dreams can come true.
2. Each of us has the kind of leadership potential we need to give hope to a dream.

Exercise Your Potential: Your Dream Life

Let's take a look at your dream life and what it might look like.

Imagine a situation where you are caught in traffic on your birthday. You're late for your own party! All your family and friends are waiting. The balloons around the room are looking a little listless. But no one is mad at you! They know how bad traffic jams can be. In fact, because it's your special day, everyone is talking about what they love the most about you and why they look forward to spending time with you. What would you want them to say?

Now, imagine you've walked in the door and your best friend

rushes up to give you a hug. They ask you to make a speech to share a story about your latest achievement. What speech would you like to make?

What's the difference between your imaginary birthday party and what you're doing right this moment, today?

What changes do you imagine for yourself in order to become that birthday person every day for the rest of your life?

What legacy do you want to have at the end of your career? At the end of your life? What do you want your friends and family to remember about you?

No matter what your answers are, take some additional time with yourself to discover your dreams. You may also want to have a journal open next to your bed and a pen ready to write down your dreams as soon as you wake so that you can explore what you really want to do with your dreams. Think about what you want to do in a world where there are no constraints, where no one says no to you.

In the next section of this book, we're going to shift our focus from Dreaming to Believing.

Now that we've taken a journey to discover our dreams and what they mean to us, we have to create a foundation. Dig our roots, as it were.

All of us have dreams, but not all of us will believe that we have the capacity to follow them and make them wholly ours, raising the roof on our potential.

Over the next few chapters, we will delve into what it takes to believe in our own power for personal growth and how we can grow the deepest roots possible so that we can generate the energy we need. In the next chapter in particular, we'll look at what it takes to believe in the gifts bestowed upon us and place our faith in each step of our journey forward.

PART III

THE BELIEVING YOU

CHAPTER 8

What Is Believing?

In northern Tanzania near the Great Rift Valley, the Iraqw peoples in Mbulu are one of the earliest communities on earth to cultivate wheat. They have large hilltop farms near a series of lakes, where the temperatures are mild and cool compared to much of Africa.

In 1938, John Stephen Akhwari was born there. He knew that his family required him to take care of the farm. As a child, he would have to run the long distances between his home and those of his neighbours to get supplies, and he'd run from the barn to the fields to bring messages to the farmhands moving through the stalks.

John was always running. Running was his gift.

It should be no surprise, then, that at thirty years old, John was asked to represent his country and compete in Mexico City in the 1968 Olympic marathon. He had just won the African Marathon Championships, competing against the best in the world.

It should have been an easy run for John, especially compared to many of his peers who weren't experienced in running through the high hills of Mbulu. But Mexico City was even higher. At an elevation of 2,240 metres above sea level, Mexico City is higher than the peak of Whistler Mountain in British Columbia, but its temperature is twice or sometimes even three times as hot in the summer.

Just before he reached the halfway point of the race, something happened to John, something bad.

He could feel his legs cramp up.

He could see the men around him struggling, their faces red.

He could sense that a few men were trying to get out of the fray and make a break for it.

All of a sudden, John could feel himself falling. He heard a crack and a snap. He felt the pain searing through his knee and his shoulder as his feet hit the ground.

John did not realize that he had dislocated his knee. John kept running.

In his mind, John brought himself back to the hillscape around his home. He saw the wheat stalks swaying in the fading summer light and felt the wind on his face. John smelled the food his mother was making for supper. In doing so, he remembered why he was there.

John kept running and running.

When he got to the finish line in the stadium an hour later than the frontrunner and Olympic gold medallist Mamo Wolde, the officials could see that John needed medical help. A television crew captured him limping down the track just after the medal ceremony had wrapped up, the last of fifty-seven runners, with eighteen others having dropped out of the race. The crowd was still cheering him on when an interviewer came up to him.

"You're clearly hurt. Why did you continue running, John?" the interviewer asked as the runner was helped onto a stretcher by the medics on the field.

"My country did not send me five thousand miles to start the race," John replied. "They sent me five thousand miles to finish the race."

Even after surgery to repair his knee, John kept on running. Two years after his fall, he placed fifth in the marathon at the Commonwealth Games in Edinburgh and fourth in the 10,000-metre race. He travelled the world with his sport, receiving the National Hero

Medal of Honor in Tanzania in 1983, and started the John Stephen Akhwari Athletic Foundation to support Tanzanian Olympic athletes. Later, John travelled as an Olympic Ambassador to the 2000 Olympics in Sydney, Australia, and to the 2008 Olympics in Beijing, China.

John still lives with his wife, children, and grandchildren on his family farm in Mbulu. But he will always be a hero to his country.

John is not a hero because he won a race.

John is a hero because he believed in his dream and stopped at nothing.

We've talked about the fact that your mindset is the most powerful activator for personal growth that you have.

I think we all know that, at the back of our minds, we have the potential to be someone we're excited to become, but we don't really believe in our own momentum because we haven't seen it happen yet.

If you don't believe in your own personal potential, then what do you actually believe in? If you don't know who you are right now, you may not know what you're capable of doing in the future. Cultivating your own beliefs and desires is an important step in activating your potential.

Having a growth mindset allows us to see everything we do as experiences in the world, rather than as setbacks. This point of view is not about overcoming hardship. Think about it this way: when John was running through Mexico City and hurt himself, he didn't focus his energy on what had gone wrong; he focused on what he had to do next to get it right.

A growth mindset makes room for our personal and professional development at its core. It is the path to dynamically choosing our own reality and being flexible so that we can adapt to what comes our way.

The reality we all face, especially when we encounter changes or hurdles in our lives, is that life requires us to keep learning and moving out of our comfort zones. We need to adopt a mindset that will help us respond in a way that doesn't shut us down in a crisis.

Without a growth mindset at work, for example, it will be very difficult to succeed and remain relevant. Without a growth mindset at home, our lives can quickly become miserable. Why? Because a fixed mindset means that there is only a single path to success, and when life's challenges change the status quo, we're going to suffer when we don't get our way. A fixed mindset makes us toddlers who are told we can't have a cookie. A growth mindset helps us remember that there are other nourishing things to eat and that we can have a cookie later on.

A growth mindset is kind of like a coin. Most people think a coin has two sides: heads and tails. We talk about flipping a coin and having it land on one of these two sides, a fifty-fifty chance of falling on heads or tails. "Call it!" we tell each other.

But we forget that a coin actually has one additional side: the edge.

When it comes to having a dream, flipping the coin and believing that heads means you win and tails means you lose is normal. That probability is where most people find themselves every day. A fixed mindset tells you that you're only going to win or lose, and there are no other options in life. If you win, you're just lucky. If you lose, you're a loser.

The chance of the coin landing on its edge is much, much smaller. Those odds, measured by scientists, are one in 6,000.[1] That's actually not bad, in probability terms. It's not one in a million. Tossing a coin and getting that edge is much easier than winning the lottery, the odds of which are, in an average standard six-number ticket in North American public lotteries, around one in 13,983,816.[2]

We never think about trying for the edge; we limit our thinking to heads or tails.

A growth mindset is kind of like a coin.

A growth mindset tells you that you can get that edge. It's a matter of belief to know that you can be the one in 6,000 who achieves their dream. Those are excellent odds. You can believe in those odds if you remember that you're betting on yourself.

And, instead of hoping and waiting for the coin to land on its edge, you can take action to ensure that it does. Flipping the coin or spinning the coin is not a strategy.

What are you doing to separate yourself from the crowd? That's *your* edge.

Mindset is also connected to the importance of mental health and wellness because it allows us to change when we're uncomfortable. It can be a small change, like saying no more often, being vulnerable, asking for help. Any change we make will create a disruption in a pattern of behaviour or thought that has served its purpose. Any change we make can put a stop to the limits we put on our future success.

When we are clear on what matters to us and can better see the life we want, we can believe in ourselves. Using a growth mindset, even within life's challenges, helps us to develop resilience: the ability to respond gracefully to whatever comes up in our world at work or in our personal lives. A growth mindset allows us to become an upgraded version of ourselves and identify the times when we are at our best. Even so, sometimes the upgraded version that we want is a bit unclear.

One day, I was having a conversation with a teenager, and he said something to me that I never wanted to hear from anyone, especially from the heart and mind of a young person. We were talking about our school hockey jerseys, and what size he needed.

"I wish I was two inches taller," he said to me. "Then all my problems would be solved."

"What do you mean?" I asked.

"I'm not tall enough to be a hockey player. I'm never going to be tall enough. I'm not six feet tall."

"You're still growing! And even if you wanted to be a basketball player, you are tall enough," I responded. "Spud Webb was five six and he was dunking the ball in the NBA. Yes, size is a factor in playing the game of hockey, but you're giving it too much importance."

"That isn't true," he said. "You have to be tall."

"Kid, the tallest, biggest, and strongest don't always make it. Why? Because there are a whole lot of other important prerequisites that must be met. You have to be strategic. You have to have heart. You need to be willing to do the work and practise every day. More than all of that, you have to be a team player. The best players have all those qualities and more."

"Really?"

"Really. And remember what the famous tennis player Arthur Ashe said: 'Start where you are. Use what you have. Do what you can.' You don't have to be tall. You have to be good. And you have to love and accept yourself. How can you raise your roof if you're not willing?"

This young man wasn't alone in his point of view. A lot of times people have this kind of fixed mindset right from the start: they're not tall enough, they're not strong enough, they're not smart enough.

But he had feet.

He had skates.

He had access to the ice.

And he believed in the potential of *other people* to become hockey players.

I didn't ask him to become a hockey star that day. Instead, I asked him to believe in his ability to take that first step, so that tomorrow, he would be able to build his skills to eventually become the person he wanted to be.

Believing: Believe in Yourself

When it comes to potential, most of us want to believe in ourselves.

And we want to believe in *each other*. We want to believe in our kids' potential, in our loved ones' potential, in our colleagues' potential.

The reality is that we don't let ourselves believe.

As a principal, I see this happening in the interactions between teachers and parents every day. Parents are worried that their children are going to fail, that they will slip behind their classmates and they won't catch up. The *New York Times* writer Jessica Grose calls these kinds of parents helicoptering hypercheckers: the kind of parents who feel that the world is now so complex and hyper-competitive that unless their kids have perfect grades and after-school activities, they won't get into the right university, which may have a permanent negative effect on their kids' potential.[3] As Grose explains, parents get into such a tizzy that they, like actress Felicity Huffman, will lie, cheat, and bribe universities into accepting their children instead of letting them rely on their own ability to reach their goals. While Huffman's situation may be an extreme one, it represents our collective fear about what our potential really is. We'd rather take shortcuts than find out if we really have what it takes.

Think about why we don't always believe in our own potential.

There is a part of Huffman's story that rings true for all of us, whether or not we have children or other loved ones we want to protect. Life can be complicated! It can be difficult. But more than that, we really cannot predict the future. We cannot predict what we will come up against, but we are going to have to come to terms with the fact that we're not supernatural. We are all just normal, everyday human beings, and that's a beautiful thing.

If we know we are human beings who have to manage changes every day, does it really help us to have a fixed mindset?

Or can we shift our perspective so that we are, at the very least, open to finding solutions that work for us?

Exercise Your Potential: Dare to Be You

Dare to be your full self.

To face obstacles effectively, we have to show up as our authentic selves. A lot has been said about the importance of showing up authentically, how living our authentic self creates a meaningful life. It's both liberating and engaging to live from our core, to dare to show up authentically. But it is also necessary in so many ways, not only because it feels right. Showing up authentically means that we're more likely to attract the things we want and value into our lives. If we don't, we'll be living a life that we don't value or believe in.

However, living authentically is also challenging, and it's a skill that we need to practise and nourish. Here's a four-step process to cultivating authenticity:

Step 1: Connect back to yourself by really understanding what you are feeling in each moment.

Too often, when we are at a meeting or driving a car or having coffee with a friend, our body is there but we are not. We are emotionally absent even when we are physically present.

So start to notice when this is happening. When you feel checked out, dare to ask yourself the following questions:

▶ How do I feel in this situation?
▶ Do I feel comfort, shame, anger, or discomfort?
▶ In what way does how I feel resonate with my own belief system?

Asking ourselves these mindful questions becomes a skill that we need to practise. In the beginning, we won't be familiar with our feelings and sensations in each moment. Dare to ask yourself what you feel, and observe what arises from becoming aware, even if it takes time.

Step 2: Tell yourself that your emotions are valid and that they are going to help you as you grow as a person.

Experience your emotions. Allow them to be present within yourself, without trying to stop. You can feel various emotions at the same time: part of you can feel happy, while another part can be curious, afraid, angry, and so on. Instead of trying to control your uncomfortable emotions, invite curiosity.

When we create space for our emotions and acknowledge them, they won't control us. Even if we are usually disconnected from our emotions, they still exist. In fact, denied emotions may show up in an intense way and influence us. If I am angry and I don't acknowledge it, for example, I may act upon my anger and shout or snap at others. Once we allow our emotions to exist, in contrast, we can change and transform them, using that emotional energy for a better purpose.

Step 3: Dare to speak your truth.

Once you acknowledge your emotions and the experiences you are going through, you can speak about them with purpose. For example, if I feel anger, I can tell my spouse or colleague that I am feeling angry right now and either ask to postpone a discussion for another time or concentrate on a new task altogether. By doing that, I know we will have a more fruitful conversation later on. I can separate my feelings of anger from my actions. My anger does not manage me, and instead I can name my feelings so that the people around me understand my choices. In this way, I can open a space for exploring our mutual work or discussions without judgment and create space for collaboration.

> When you dare to be yourself, it's easier to tell yourself that you believe in your potential.

Whether you have found a way to address your own obstacles head-on or you have one that is unresolved, your awareness of your own potential is key. Did you stand up to a boss who said inappropriate things? Or did you bite your tongue and replay the scenario over and over in your mind for weeks?

Step 4: Write down your edge.

Be honest, because we all have an edge, and somewhere in you, you know exactly what that edge is.

What do you have in your personality, your skill set, your experience, or your dreams that sets you apart?

Where in your life are *you* that one in 6,000?

You can do hard things. You have faced challenges in the past and gotten past them. If you're reading this book, you're still here, willing and able to take a hard look at how you deal with difficulties. You have an edge.

Knowing that, you also have permission to have a growth mindset. You have permission to keep learning, growing, and being the person you believe that you are today.

Every day that you live on this earth builds upon what you learned yesterday, and you can trust yourself to create things and change direction tomorrow.

You'll never know what's possible until you believe in your potential to become the next, better version of yourself. When you dare to be yourself, it's easier to tell yourself that you believe in your potential.

In daring to bring ourselves fully to every task we take on, with our full experiences and our thoughts, feelings, and emotions, we can live a more authentic life. Being open to a holistic approach to our own lives will create space for deeper personal connections and better solutions to emerge, at work and at home.

CHAPTER 9

Trust Yourself to Fall

I was in Rome for the vacation of a lifetime. I travelled there to see Italy, connect with the history and culture, and feed my appetite with some spaghetti.

While Rome is known for the Colosseum, the Pantheon, St. Peter's Basilica, and many more historical and architectural wonders, on my visit there several years ago, it also became known to us as the home for Karl's Great Fall. Over my lunchtime meal, I became Rome's main attraction.

While waiting for my spaghetti in a beautiful, savoury-smelling restaurant, the legs of my chair buckled under my weight. After hitting the floor with a big thud, everyone, including the restaurant staff and my family members, ran over to assist me.

I wasn't physically injured, but I found myself swimming in an ocean of embarrassment. I got up off the floor, because that is what you do when you fall. In fact, I followed the advice I give my children and grandchildren when I teach them how to skate.

"What do you do when you fall? You get up!"

My great fall in Rome reminded me that everyone learns how to fall and how to get up before really learning how to skate. Think about it for a moment: if you fear falling, you will not conquer skating. Similarly, if you fear making mistakes or failing at life's tasks, you will be faced with some great challenges, too.

But in the moment, I was grateful because I was given a new chair and a healthy serving of spaghetti, a serving bigger than my plate. It was supersized. The server wanted me to be happy and I was. After downing my big lunch, I was served a wonderfully tasty dessert, all on the house.

I guess there are benefits to falling.

But there are also benefits to finding a better chair to sit on in the first place.

The problem many of us have is that we hate taking risks that may not pay off. But we hate the idea of failing ourselves even more. It's kind of the same as trimming back the branches on a growing tree. When we're making that first cut, we feel nervous. We're not sure where we should shear off a branch, especially if it has grown up through a fence or some wiring. At the same time, if we don't take a hard look at what we're doing and trust where we're going, we may just be encouraging rapid overgrowth instead of a beautiful acacia.

> The problem many of us have is that we hate taking risks that may not pay off. But we hate the idea of failing ourselves even more.

Most of us second-guess almost everything we do, even when we are experts. Many of us do the exact opposite of what our intuition tells us is necessary at any given moment. We just don't trust our own finely honed intuition. We follow, rather than lead, even within our own homes, our cars, our vacation choices.

Instead, we need to trust our intuition, and ourselves, if we're going to have any chance at all of believing in our potential. It is only through self-trust that we can begin to correct our course.

I have learned a great deal about falling down and getting up from my brother. In the mid-nineties, he moved to British Columbia. He had the clothes on his back and the shoes on his feet, but an almost empty wallet in his pocket. He had very few possessions, but plenty of drive, will, and determination. There was a lot more inside him than what was in his wallet.

Job hunting was his first priority, and he quickly landed a job sanding drywall on a construction site. It was dusty and dirty, and when the job triggered his asthma, he moved on. Someone gave my brother a tip about another company that was hiring. My brother called and arranged a meeting the next day.

"Can you hang doors?" the contractor asked.

"Yes!" my brother enthusiastically responded. When you are in desperation mode, you can do anything and all things, from flying a kite to flying a rocket to the moon.

"How about windows?"

"I can do that, too!"

Shortly after being hired, he ran into a friend and told him about his new employer.

"Oh, you got hired by Peanuts." His friend nodded and smiled.

"Peanuts? What do you mean? His name is Dan."

"You'll see."

On payday, my brother looked at the numbers on his paycheque and discovered why his new employer was nicknamed Peanuts.

My brother did not go nuts over his salary. He looked at it this way: he was learning a lot, even though he wasn't making a lot of money. He figured that was the price he had to pay for learning how he wanted to make a living. He learned to make good out of a bad situation.

Later in his life, my brother moved back to Ontario. He heard that the TTC, the Toronto Transit Commission, was hiring, and he joined the line to complete an application for a well-paid job with benefits. When he reached the front of the line, the staff member who greeted him asked him a question that can be taken only a certain way, especially by a person of colour.

"Can you climb trees?" the man asked, looking my brother up and down.

Asking a Black person if they can climb trees isn't much different from using the N-word in some circles. Call it a lightning rod for a major conflict.

"Yes, I can climb trees," my brother answered with a big smile on his face.

There are some people I know, and you might know some, too, who would not be smiling after fielding that kind of question. They would come out swinging like a baseball player. *Bang! There it goes. Over and out!* I am not advocating violence here, but coming up against racial hatred leaves many of us feeling like we're dying inside.

The TTC staff member looked at my brother in silence. After a few moments passed, he spoke.

"The branches of trees are getting in the way of buses, street cars, and subway trains," the man said. "We need someone who isn't afraid of heights and who can use clippers, a saw, and a chain-saw to give the trees a haircut. Do you think you can do that?"

My brother got the job as a tree barber. Would he have been successful if he'd started World War III right there in the TTC human resources office?

My brother had the wherewithal to control his emotions and to accept the possibility that he wouldn't get the job. In fact, at every step in his career, my brother kept his eyes on the prize rather than on his likelihood of failure. He didn't let his initial lack of skills get in the way of trying out a new profession, and he didn't let a fear of being racialized stop him from getting a better job later on.

When you have a strong belief in your abilities and yourself, you tend to deal with sensitive situations in healthy ways. My brother was able to differentiate what he can do and what he is able to do from the person he is. In his mind, he separated the TTC staff member's question from his own conception of his personhood. He followed his intuition, stayed the course, and believed in his ability to reach his potential.

Believing: Over-Correction

When I was a teacher, I'd ask students a lot of questions. More often than not, when they didn't know the answers, they'd guess. They didn't want to be wrong, of course. When they were told the right answer, they'd over-correct themselves trying to be more right.

Adults do the same thing. Research in neuropsychology shows that people are more likely to over-correct themselves when they are right than when they are wrong.[1]

Why do we do this? The same research shows that people will go over and over answers in their heads so they can be a little bit more confident in what they're saying. We do this again and again, only to fall back on the idea that we are completely failing. This pattern is ingrained in all of us. And the same is true when we're faced with the opinions of others. Even when other people are incorrect, we believe them before we trust ourselves! We keep on looking for ways that we're wrong and ways that we don't match up with others' expectations.

In essence, we want to receive feedback that tells us we're wrong, not right.

That's the reason why we need to get really powerful at falling, failing, and making everyday mistakes.

In the classroom, I notice my students being afraid to fail all the time.

Some students don't raise their hands when they're asked to contribute.

Some students look over other kids' shoulders to check if they have better answers.

Some students don't ask questions in case they look silly.

Some students get nervous and anxious and ask to go to the bathroom rather than participate.

We all do these things sometimes. Think about your own life. Are there little habits that you've picked up to get out of actually having to come up with the right answers?

The problem with thinking this way is that it is when we stop or give up or cheat that we're really falling off our figurative chairs. Failing is actually a big part of the learning process because determination is our best friend. Do you know how to skate? Skating requires you to warm up, fall down, and take small steps. Skating is one of the only skills you can learn where you are guaranteed to literally fall down over and over again.

When we do science experiments in school classrooms, for example, it's equally important to find out what works and what doesn't. When we add water to citric acid and bicarbonate of soda, it bubbles and fizzes, and the kids start to smile. When we add water to coloured oil, the oil floats on the top of the water, and the kids smile again. In both experiments, we add water to something new and different, but neither is a failure or a success: they just bring forward different results.

We need to see what happens when we try. Just like when my brother tried to be a drywaller, a door installer, and a TTC tree trimmer, we can actually achieve different results with the same inputs: authenticity, commitment, and an ability to take simple risks.

Think about why believing that we are going to be okay if we fail is a massive part of making sure we can reach our potential.

Think about why we can't experiment without experiencing failure, and we can't learn without failing.

Think about why we have to trust that we may actually know what's right for us.

So what else can we learn about my brother's ability to trust himself?

Why was he okay with failing?

My brother didn't let his emotions stand in the way of taking risks.

Now, let me be clear. We are all human beings, and having emotions is a huge benefit to us. I would never advocate for any person to let go of their emotions. This is important! Many books on personal growth try to get people to set aside their emotions in order to make more logical and rational decisions. That is not what I'm saying here.

We need to recognize our emotions, especially in situations that are new to us, so that we can measure risks more easily.

Research shows that the emotions we use to make decisions might be different from what we expect.[2]

When we are either happy or angry, it's easy to make a decision. Think about a time when you were really happy and someone asked you a question, even something simple such as where you'd like to go for dinner on your birthday. Would you hesitate in telling your friend what you'd like to do on your birthday? When I was in Italy, happily touring around, I knew for certain I wanted to have a spaghetti dinner. There was absolutely no question about conveying that happy desire to my family. When we're angry, we're also very certain. Think about a time when you were presented with an unfair situation at work or school. Did you hesitate for even a moment before deciding what to do next?

When people are happy or angry, they know exactly how they feel and what they want to do, whether or not these decisions will serve them. That's because, in these two emotional states, information is less relevant to getting the decision made.

The opposite is true when we experience either fear or hope. In these emotional states, we are uncertain about what matters to us. These are the states in which we're more likely to want information, to dig into life's details, to process many different options, and to seek out professional help.

Fear, however, is our worst enemy when it comes to making decisions. When we are stuck in a fear state, our higher-order cognitive functions shut down due to physical and emotional stress.

Let's apply these ideas to my brother when he was hoping to get a job at the TTC. Initially, he was in a state of emotional hope. He didn't have all of the information he needed to be successful, but he knew he was going to try. When he thought that he was facing racism, he probably felt a sudden mix of anger and fear. Instead of moving into decision mode immediately, spurred by his anger, he waited to see what was going to happen next.

Exercise Your Potential: Changing Direction

Your belief in yourself has to be stronger than the obstacles you're facing.

To do this, you need to tell yourself that you believe in your potential and actually mean it.

Let's develop a practice around your belief in yourself.

Think about a very specific time in your past where you thought you had to change direction because, all of a sudden, your life circumstances were suddenly wildly different. Think about a time when you failed an important test at school, or when you were awarded a promotion for a job you felt was out of your league. Perhaps you were audited for your taxes, or you found yourself in an unfamiliar part of a new town when you were travelling. Maybe a loved one became ill and you were the only one who could help. Write down the bare facts of what happened during that life experience. Describe the situation.

How did it feel to be in a situation that was so uncertain?

What did you decide to change about your life, your work, or your schedule when you first found out about this challenge?

How did this change affect you, emotionally, intellectually, and physically? Did you feel scared? Powerful? Confused?

Change it up, now.

What about a time in your life where you were presented with a challenge and you *didn't* switch direction? Describe that situation.

Did you miss an opportunity?

Or did staying on your path feel right to you then and now? There is no right answer.

Most importantly, for both situations, knowing that you've changed a lot since that time, what would you do differently if you encountered similar situations right now?

Read your answers back to yourself and then write down a challenge that you are facing right now. What are all the choices you have?

Turning the page to the next chapter, we're going to discover that it is up to each of us to build our own safety net in the process of reaching our potential. To remain motivated throughout all of the challenges that we face in life, we must be able to find peace amidst the chaos and work through our most difficult vulnerabilities.

CHAPTER 10

Feel Safe Within

Sometimes, it feels like our lives and our careers are just too difficult to reconcile.

In 2024, Gallup's *State of the Global Workplace*[1] reported that only 6 percent of Japanese workers felt engaged at work. Employee engagement happens when people are motivated to do their jobs and are content with their level of achievement and the meaning of their tasks relative to their own value system.

It's a better situation in the rest of the world, but not by much. The same survey says that there is a global workforce engagement average of only 23 percent.

Engagement isn't just about performing at work. Gallup says that people who are engaged are emotionally, mentally, and physically healthier. They know that their lives have potential. They are thriving and well. They are taking action.

As an old Japanese proverb states: "Vision without action is a daydream. Action without vision is a nightmare."

People who are not engaged are taking the actions they are *paid* to take, not necessarily the ones they *want* to take. They aren't working from their own vision; they are working to support someone else's dream. None of these people are actually reaching their potential because they feel so disconnected from their own selves that they're simply showing up without caring about what happens next.

So why don't people feel engaged?

We know that it has a little, or maybe a lot, to do with power. Women feel less engaged at work. People who immigrate to a new country feel less engaged. So do people of colour and those living with disabilities and difference.

That's why, a lot of the time, we see ourselves as the problem. We blame ourselves for not having all the answers and not having a vision to change our future. We also think we're alone in our feelings. We think we're the only ones who are discontent, when in fact those of us who are disengaged are among the majority.

To feel safe and secure in who we are, we need community, and, more than that, we need to feel deeply connected to other people in order to balance out what we have and don't have. Community isn't just about wanting to do the same things, it's about recognizing that we're all different and yet all connected, perhaps more than we think.

I have a mentor, Dr. Jim. He just turned eighty. I met him the year I started my teaching at the York Board of Education, when I replaced him at Arlington Middle School. Over our careers, he moved up the ladder from teacher to principal to superintendent, and when he became my boss, we built a strong friendship. Whenever I meet with him, even today, I bring my journal with me because I know I'm going to learn something. I want to make sure that I can capture the best parts of our conversation, to savour his words for days, weeks, and years after we connect. He is someone in my life who always brings knowledge and experience to the table. He makes me feel connected to my profession and renews my spirit of engagement in my work coaching and teaching.

The organizational psychologist Edgar Schein, who was a professor at MIT in his prime, advised companies that the psychological safety of employees—namely, having enough of a sense of personal identity and integrity to go ahead with changes—was crucial to business success.[2] Psychological safety is a key part of being connected in the workforce, the feeling that others have your back when you're having a bad day. Schein predicted that, without it, job satisfaction and organizational commitment would go down, and absenteeism, turnover, knowledge loss, and advantage-taking would be the norm in companies.

Schein argued that understanding human relationships and solving what he saw as the problems of power, influence, and hierarchy would make a working group safe, comfortable, and productive.

In fact, what Schein advised was that building the conditions for platonic forms of love, the kind of love you share with your best friends, would serve companies and employees alike. That way, people would feel like they could be themselves at work, finding their own vision within and being confident on the outside.

But I think that if we want to feel safe so we can reach our potential, we actually have to go in an entirely different direction. We're all likely to feel vulnerable and unsafe in life.

Every young person with whom I have worked arrived into this world with unlimited potential. I see it every day. I want *them* to see it, feel it, and hear it, to know that they matter and that they can each raise their own roof. I love to hear these words from their mouths: "I believe in my potential."

I remember one young person who arrived in my office with a lot more than potential. What I mean is that he came to me filled to the brim with out-of-control anger. It was regularly on display like a sale sign in a store on Boxing Day, hard to miss because it was written in big, bold, red letters.

This student's anger was a major roadblock to reaching his potential on many levels. When he went into a rage, we would have to activate staff members who were trained to manage him.

When he was that upset, he was no longer a person; he was anger personified.

We're all likely to feel vulnerable and unsafe in life.

"Why is it that you're so angry all of the time?" I asked him after a difficult incident in the classroom.

"My dad always tells me he's coming to see me, and then he never shows up. It sets off my anger and sends me to a place that grows more anger," he replied, describing his most vulnerable trigger.

The empty promises his father made hurt him so badly that, one day, my student became so upset that he ripped off his golf shirt and tore it apart. (Even today, many years later, the sight of him standing there without his shirt on remains my image of anger.) On this same day, he made me cry, too; you don't make it as an educator until you shed some tears. I felt helpless, not hopeless, when he cried out my name.

"Mr. Subban, help me!"

In this moment, he wasn't somebody else's kid. He was mine. He was mine. He will always be mine.

In my work as a coach and an educator, I see the same patterns happening, especially if children are a part of an excluded social group. Whether they're in the classroom or in the dressing room, we want our children to be safe, not only physically but also mentally. But that doesn't always happen, especially because children are intrinsically vulnerable. Bullying happens. Failure happens. Domestic violence happens. And it's not always easy to show up every day to learn when we feel unsafe, uncared for, and without a sense of what to do next.

Believing: Feel Safe

We may not all be as angry as my student, but it is clear what can happen when we don't feel safe in our own skin.

There are many life experiences that we, even as adults, may feel triggered by. These triggers may be visible or invisible. We may know exactly why we're angry or upset: we have conflict at home or at work that makes us feel small. Or we may not even be aware of our barriers to psychological safety. These may arise from forgotten memories of feeling isolated, alone, or worried, memories that we can't easily access but that affect our belief in ourselves.

If the story of Japanese workers holds any weight, it's because we all know what it feels like to be disconnected and unsure of what to do next. We've all been in a place where we don't know if we can be who we truly are in front of each other, especially when we're at work and we're supposed to be proving our worth every day.

What can you do to make yourself feel safer believing in yourself?

What can you do to make yourself feel safer trying out new things?

What can you do to make yourself feel more engaged in your own life?

Think about one thing you can do today to feel safer than yesterday.

I have three items of symbolic significance on my wall behind my desk. The first item is a picture of a parent with a baby. It's a reminder that caring is an essential part of what I do and what we all need to do for each other. Sharing our dreams and desires with those we care most about deeply enhances the relationships we have and gives us a focus beyond our daily activities.

The second item is a picture of Terry Fox. His story is a constant inspiration. Knowing that a person can meet and exceed their potential even under the most difficult conditions is something that my students need to hear about.

The third item is Stanley Cup winner Gerry Cheevers's goalie mask. The mask is kind of scary. It's called the "puck stopper," and it's covered with painted-on black-and-red hospital stitches, symbolizing all the pucks that hit his mask. Even so, the mask seems to smile, with its turned-up mouth.

And it's that mask that is the most important symbol of all, because every child comes to school with a mask on, and it is the job of the educator to get behind the mask of the child.

As children, who we are shines. It shines from our faces, from our bold choices to trust strangers and to hold the hands of our best friends in the park. When they smile, laugh, sing a song, or dance to music, children are who they are, unashamedly. But over time, that light of trust can disappear, and it does for almost all of us, whether or not we experienced real trauma.

When we grow up, we can lose our way, our purpose and joy. Our sense of safety and security may not be there anymore, or it feels like it can be taken away at any moment. Like those workers in Japan, we're just not feeling it.

That's why we all put on our masks.

We have this feeling that if we take off our masks, we will be exposed and vulnerable.

Well, if I tell people about what's really going on with me, then they'll have ammunition to use against me, we think to ourselves.

We worry that everyone's going to find out who we really are.

We worry about what's going to happen when everyone finds out. Will we get shamed? Will we get treated poorly? Will we be made to feel embarrassed? Then we start making lists, thinking about all the possible ways that things can go wrong.

Part of the problem is that we buy into a society that says that we're not allowed to show our feelings. Many, if not most, people believe that taking their mask off would be more painful than keeping it on.

As James Baldwin once wrote, "Love takes off the masks that we fear we cannot live without and know we cannot live within."[3]

Sometimes it makes sense to not face the pain. Maybe we are not emotionally resourced enough: our home, social systems, and health care systems aren't there for us. We are lacking safety and comfort. We are overwhelmed. It makes sense to cloak ourselves with a mask to help us get through crises.

The way we build safety and trust is by first acknowledging where we really are.

Not where we want to say we're at.

Not what people want to hear.

Where we *really are.*

I think if you constantly believe that the worst is yet to come, you may operate out of a very limited scope of *how to be* in the world.

Where to be in the world.

Each person has so much more going on with them than they actually let people see. And so, if we tell ourselves that no one cares, then we operate as if feeling safe is pointless because no one is going to get what we really feel, no matter what. And until we build connections with the people around us so that we recognize and realize we're not alone, that's not going to change.

Exercise Your Potential: Take Off Your Mask

If we want to really feel safe, we have to create the conditions in which we can trust ourselves.

We don't have to prove or demonstrate anything to anyone else or continue to ask others to assist us. That's exhausting.

Understanding that we have a mask means understanding that we are not alone and that other people care. It means understanding that we're valuable and worth something. It allows us to take a step towards identifying who we really are connected to, building more alignment between our real self and our real values.

We have to create our own safety and trust within ourselves first.

Taking off your mask is the first step towards self-trust. Remember that action without vision is a nightmare. Right now, you're going to develop your own personal vision so you can take action with more confidence and clarity, and so can you feel fully yourself. All the answers to your vision are inside of you. It's just a matter of extracting them, like magic.

Find a quiet, comfortable space to think about your future. As you read through the following questions, take a moment to close your eyes and truly envision who you are and who you want to become. Keep in mind that you can always revisit these activities with each of your dreams and goals. The point of the exercise is to become clear about a vision that is currently of importance to you.

As you think about your future, consider the following questions:

1. Why is having a clear vision of the future important to you?
2. How can you find joy, happiness, and importance through this vision?

3. Who are the people benefiting from what you are doing? Who is a part of it?

4. Where does the vision take place? Describe the sights, sounds, and emotions you might experience if you follow your vision.

5. Will this vision of yourself provide you with the ability to take off your mask and be your full self?

Explore the possibilities. Write, draw, or record yourself answering the questions above. This isn't the time to self-edit, it's the time to explore all the possibilities of your future. In as much detail as possible, imagine your future and the vision you would like to incorporate into your life.

Look for themes. Review what you have written, drawn, or created and look for any themes that may have emerged. You can go back and either note, circle, highlight, or underline the significant words or phrases, pictures, and images that are important to you. Evaluate what may be driving these thoughts. Continue to hone your vision and identify the most significant elements that can create a clear picture. Think of the emotions that would feel true to you in the situation. Think of actions that fulfill the vision of your future. Then take all this information and create a list that highlights the best of the best from your own words and images.

Simplify the vision. As you review the themes identified, look for patterns. It's okay to get rough ideas and revisit them again even after you have them written down. The more you can make your vision simple and full of life, the easier it becomes to share. It can also be used to help select opportunities, activities, and directions that bring you closer to fulfilling that vision. As you clarify this vision in simple terms, be clear about what the future will become. The more concise the vision, the better it will move you in the right direction. Once you have this language identified, simplify, simplify, simplify. It is a craft to simplify your message, and once you do it, it becomes even clearer to implement. This will make it easier for you to remember it and incorporate it into all aspects of your life.

Make your vision visible. Just because you have it done, it doesn't mean it *is* done. Now is the time for you to display it in a way that will continually remind you about the vision you are striving toward. Select a prominent place to display your vision. This may be a specific location, or a place in the forefront of your mind. You can even take a picture of your vision to keep close at hand. Share it with others who can also impact your vision. Keep in mind, a visible vision may or may not be visible to others. It does, however, have to be visible to you.

The power of a vison is the magic that comes with it.

Once your vision is clear, it will keep presenting itself to you. The vision wants to come to fruition; therefore, your job is to allow it to manifest and become a reality.

Barriers aren't always imaginary. There are always going to be authentically challenging setbacks along the way towards un-leashing our full potential. To deal with adversity, we can either embrace our own leadership, or we can fail to lead. There are no other choices.

Take advantage of your own awareness that life is going to continue to have its challenges, whether or not you work hard and get better at fulfilling your potential. By understanding this, you can act on your personal values and rise above these setbacks.

Whatever you're facing should never become bigger than the dream you're chasing.

CHAPTER 11

Say Yes to Yourself

One day while he was cooking and running around the kitchen trying to manage a number of tasks simultaneously, my brother placed his cell phone down.

Out of sight and out of mind. He had no idea where it was.

My brother retraced his steps in the house. He knew that he had been doing household chores and that I had also picked him up to run errands. It had been a long day for all of us.

It was already the dark of night by the time he used a relative's phone to call me and ask me to check my car. After I searched the interior of my car, rooting under the seats and calling his number again and again, we remained in the dark. No phone.

The clock was ticking close to midnight, and I was running on empty. So, when he asked me to pick him up to drive to the last destination we had visited together to search for his phone, my body was saying no, but the brotherly love in my heart was saying yes. After some tired driving to that location, no luck was to be had. Again and again, we made phone calls that no one answered.

My brother was very sad. I didn't tell him that I had been planning to get him a new phone. I wanted it to be a surprise. But what I didn't know was that our youngest brother had also purchased a new phone and was planning to surprise our brother with it. There were a lot of hidden opportunities at play.

Despite our collective efforts, no new phone was required. Before the sun came up the next day, I saw my brother's name and phone number pop up on an incoming call. My brother couldn't wait to share the good news. He had found his phone.

Shockingly, he had placed his phone in the freezer of his fridge. He found it when he opened his freezer to take out food to prepare breakfast.

Because the phone was in freezer, my brother couldn't hear it ringing. I had called several times, and it would go to voice mail.

We've all had the experience of losing or misplacing things. We've all faced feelings of disappointment and adversity. But even when we are overwhelmed, we need to take time to ourselves and slow down. That's why, even though there are several life lessons from this true story, I believe that to reach our potential, we must be like the phone in the freezer.

In the face of adversity and disappointment, we need to be calm and cool. Remember that the sun or moon is always shining behind the darkest clouds.

We need to turn off the outside noise and turn down the feeling of sadness within.

We need to know when to end the conversation and when to open the door for others to see where and who you are. Self-doubt is a cage that imprisons the potential in you and me.

How do we use the gifts that we've been given to the best of our potential?

One asset is the subconscious, known to some as the safe harbour of our ego. For most of us, the subconscious is the nerve centre of who we are, and in some ways, it's like the operating system of human life. We greatly appreciate that we do not need to tell computers every single command in detail in order for them to complete a function that we desire. The same is true for how we move through our days and express our unique humanity.

When we train our subconscious to look for what is going wrong instead of what is going right, we end up having issues that we can't solve. That's because we often tell ourselves, again and again, the reasons why we have to choose the path of least resistance, and all of these reasons have to do with the outside noise around us—the noise that tells us we can't do what we really want to do.

"No, I can't dance that often, even as a hobby, because it will take away my focus and I will make less money."

"No, there are barriers in my way to losing weight because I have an illness that decreases my energy."

"No, I can't get ahead at work because Sharon in Human Resources doesn't like me."

We can, however, choose a different way of framing the issue.

"Yes, I can dance often and share my love for the practice if I teach a children's class on the weekends to see if I really want to change careers."

"Yes, I have an illness that decreases my energy, and I know I will feel better if I work with a physiotherapist who might be able to design some exercises that work well for me so that I can eventually recover."

"Yes, I know that Sharon in Human Resources doesn't like me, and because of that, I'm going to seek out a mentor in my department who will act as my career ally."

Believing: Moving from "No, But" to "Yes, And"

In switching the perspective from "no, but" to "yes, and," we get to choose differently. We can explore a whole new group of ideas by telling ourselves new stories about using the gifts that we have been given.

Think about this every time you feel that "no, but" coming on: Is this the hill you want to die on?

Pick your battles. Maybe there really is no battle unless we create one. How do you want to make choices? How will you find your freedom?

> ### Self-doubt is a cage that imprisons the potential in you and me.

How can you turn off the outside noise and say yes to yourself?

Your value, your self-worth, is not a reflection of your output, your service, your skills, or anything external. Your self-value *is* a reflection of your values and how your measure and judge yourself against them. As we now know, most times, these values have been "given" to us. It is more likely that we didn't choose them than we did!

Knowing that, how do you choose to see yourself now?

Neither our value nor our self-worth should be measured against outside noise.

This is the case even though most of us do it. It's just silly. Plain and simple. Just like how we discussed that courage is very unique from person to person, so is our personal potential. By showing us what they can accomplish, others people can reflect to us what our own potential *may* be. That's cool when we hold it that way. That's inspiring and being inspired. If *they* can do *that*, then what am *I* capable of?! Most likely, it's not exactly the same thing. But remember, before that person accomplished whatever it was they did for the first time in their own lives, they were also wondering if they would be able to do it.

Perspective is the gift we need, yet again.

If we're feeling not enough, or not capable, we're also often afraid others are going to "out us." If you're in that kind of internal-judgment machine, you're going to be projecting that. You're going to launch yourself into a black hole of despair. But here is the thing. We can step away from jealousy and negative self-judgment and embrace being inspired by others!

And we don't have to win.

There really is no winning in comparison to others. Not really. In life, when we make choices, we are simply proving to ourselves what we are capable of, but we might measure what we have achieved in the terms of the achievements of others. Instead, consider acknowledging your *effort* and *not the outcome*. What might that look like? How would your day, choices, and life look from there? How might that feel?

We make certain choices based upon our levels of awareness: awareness of self and awareness of the world around us. Most significantly, we make choices based upon what we believe our options to be. What do I believe? I have asked myself this many times, and I still do pretty much every day. It helps me to understand, be aware of, and own who I am choosing to be. It can also help me to remember that we are truly *limitless*.

Instead of leaning into self-doubt, we all need to be our own biggest fan. Every time we tell ourselves that we're not capable of reaching our potential, we're doing ourselves a disservice. As a principal, I've witnessed that those of us who grow up in unstable homes will face this challenge more than others. But the world is lining up to take shots at us, so we can't do the same to ourselves.

The trick to cutting out the noise permanently is to begin to extend love to yourself.

There are a couple of words that I wanted my children and students to feel and know when I was raising, leading, and teaching them.

One of these words is *love*. Young people don't care about what you want them to do unless they know and feel that you care about them.

Love is the glue that makes relationships work and that makes our children work confidently, for longer, and with more determination.

There is another word that every young person must know: the word *no*. *No* has always been a tool in my parenting and education toolbox. When parents don't know or use it, our children don't learn it. When parents don't use it, young people don't learn to work through it. I said no to a lot of children because I cared about them. When the word *no* is foreign to our children, they can struggle to reach their potential.

Why?

The word *love* and the word *no* are related to one another. Both of these words lead to self-belief and self-care when we apply them to our own lives. We have to feel loved to believe in our own potential. And we need the word *no* to set our own boundaries. We have to learn how to say no to others so that we can say yes to ourselves.

I heard the word *no* from my parents. My dad's no was delivered in the form of a look. My five children heard the word *no*, and sometimes it was the only word they would hear from me in a day, and I adopted the "no" look, which they learned to understand very well. Learning to read body language and the looks on my face helped them to be safe and to understand that it was okay to set boundaries. Young people need boundaries, and saying no reinforces them, especially when we do so in a loving way.

To grow to our maximum potential, we must operate outside our comfort zone. When you become comfortable with being un-comfortable, that's when you are growing and getting ahead in life and school. But we must also be able to lovingly put the brakes on things that stretch us too far. We have to be able to reserve the energy we have for what will truly raise our roof.

A friend of mine, another school principal, shared a situation with me that shines the spotlight on the benefits of saying no. It was after the first month of the school year, and because of declining enrolment, she was tasked with reorganizing the middle school classes. Most students were okay with the changes, except one. This student did not want to be separated from her teacher and classmates. The young middle school student became the leader of the opposition to the principal and her new school organization. She was suffering from separation anxiety to the highest degree. She organized an army of adults to make presentations to the principal on her behalf. The principal did not want to give in to her, because once you give in to one family, you will be pressured to do the same for others. A no had to be a solid no, not a maybe or a yes.

The principal did not move away from her leadership decision. She made decisions in the best interest of the school and for all the students and families. In this case, she saw more than the others that this is what leaders do. The change is not what the student wanted, but it was the very thing she needed to reach her potential. Learning to work through change and adversity and being uncomfortable are essential to achieving to your highest potential. Before the Christmas holidays, the student walked into the principal's office wearing a big smile.

"Miss, I love my new teacher and classmates. I normally give Ferrero Rocher as a gift, but I am giving you Godiva chocolate. One of the most expensive brands."

It pays to say no, and everyone benefits—receiver and sender.

We either embrace ourselves or resist ourselves. There is no neutral way of going about life. It's time to choose. The choice you make here and now is akin to the intention that you set for yourself. Again, it's not easy, but it is a simple choice: resist yourself or embrace yourself, and all your flaws, inconveniences, and challenges, for what you are. It seems to me that for many of us, embracing, accepting, and ultimately loving ourselves is the only real work that we have.

True love is based on understanding, trust, and respect and not simply on transient emotions, be they internal or external. Love is being in balance and in harmony with the self, each other, and the universe. Love dwells within us all. It is our very nature when we are not in fear.

Perhaps the opposite of being "in fear" is being "in love"? To be alive and in love with yourself is to grow.

> We either embrace ourselves or resist ourselves.
> There is no neutral way of going about life.

When I am about to make a choice, if the answer happens to be less obvious to me in the given moment, I will consider if the choice is *loving*.

In these moments, ask yourself:

1. Am I loving myself by making this choice?
2. Am I being loving to others as I make this choice?

The answers to these questions are simple but not always easy. We might think it should be easy to make choices this way, but more often than we might think, it is not.

Why might we choose to not make a loving choice?

Why indeed? There really isn't a good answer here, no easy way to defend or justify our choices. How do we choose to align with our spirit here, our true sense and knowing of ourselves?

In fact, for me, the very definition of being alive is being in growth.

Everything in our lives, in our experience of life, pushes us to grow. At times, it seems like an evolutionary imperative. We grow or we die, or perhaps it's more like we grow until we die. Or until we don't, like we have no other choice.

We always have a choice. Choosing not to grow would be akin to choosing not to breathe. One can make that choice, but the outcome is predictable, and in this case, the same. Simply put from my perspective, growth, and the force powering it, is a given and a constant. It just is.

The *real* choice, the *primary* choice that we all make, then, is the choice to resist growth or to embrace it. Either way, grow we will! There really is no middle ground here that I have ever found, though I admit to having tried to find one many a time.

So what do *you* choose?

If we choose to resist, which most of us do at least some of the time, we will still grow, but our path may be long and arduous and full of discomfort and possibly suffering. Though this road, like all roads, can lead us home, we may just run out of time and find little joy in the journey.

Choosing to embrace growth by no means ensures that we will avoid discomfort and suffering along the way, but it does ensure that our path will be more fluid and filled with potential to experience the joy of our growth more fully.

So, see what you are willing or able to choose. But in doing so, play with imagining that you might actually have no limits. That you can be in love with yourself and what you choose. That you might actually already be free!

Exercise Your Potential: What Will You Put in the Freezer?

It is important to understand and celebrate the person we were as well as the one we are becoming.

Change means we are continually evolving with each experience and encounter. The person we once were may not be the person we are today, however those experiences from the past have influenced us in some way. There is value in celebrating the foundation we were planted from—each and every time we define foundation.

We may no longer be the same person we once were, but we can honour, appreciate, and allow our foundation to evolve in order to grow into the person we are meant to be.

What can you see hidden in the picture of yourself right now?

The picture that I see of myself is quite different from what I was at nineteen years old, and even different from who I was a decade ago. I'm alive. I'm creative. I'm focused on teaching and developing leaders, wherever they are in their leadership journey. And this quest for continual growth isn't over. I'm not sure who I will become and where the journey will take me. This is all a part of our life's process.

Each of us has the opportunity to find our focus and to become the person we're meant to be.

How do we do this?

Think about what you need to put in the freezer so that you can say yes to yourself.

Our starting point is to identify the items that can be removed from our plate, those unnecessary tasks, items, beliefs, or whatever it may be. We start by taking away in order to focus on what is important, to get to the heart of what we want to achieve in life. You've probably heard this phrase a lot before: Just because it's urgent, doesn't mean it is important.

The point of identifying what you need to put in the freezer is to reduce extra activities that can consume our everyday lives. This means that we can intentionally let go of responsibilities or tasks that are unnecessary or overwhelming.

Now you are positioning yourself for only the best opportunities that come your way.

But before you add anything to your potential goals, ask yourself these questions to ensure that you keep to your intentional focus.

1. If I take on a new task, in what ways is it getting me closer to reaching my potential?
2. If I take on a new task, in what ways is it taking me further away from reaching my potential?
3. Am I doing this because I'm saying yes to myself, or because I feel like I have to?
4. Let your answers be your guide.

The art of saying yes to yourself is to take the time and space to do what you need so that the full answers to these questions can come to you.

CHAPTER 12

Dig Deep Roots

My father's father came from the subcontinent of India. My mother's relatives came from the continent of Africa.

It's no wonder I love to cook.

My parents love cooking, and so I grew up doing the same. My brother also loves cooking. Cooking is not a job. Cooking is not an arduous task. Cooking is not a burden. Cooking is something that I love to do, and that I want to do for my family every day. I especially love making a meal for my grandchildren.

During the coldest month of the year not too long ago, my family doctor requested that I come to see him on a Saturday morning. I had completed my yearly physical and he wanted to go over the results. My life changed when he dropped a bomb.

"You have diabetes," he said.

"What do you mean?" I asked. "I'm feeling okay."

"Well, you may be okay right now, but I want to make sure you stay that way. Tell me a bit about your family history, Karl."

I started to think. I knew that my grandmother was diabetic, and so was my aunt, my mom's sister. Both of them had acquired diabetes in adulthood. The doctor used this history to help me manage my medical condition.

I decided to take control of my diabetes full on. I made the decision, in that moment, to change my lifestyle by exercising regularly, managing stress effectively, and reducing sugar in my diet.

My family tree is not incidental to my self-image and personal values. It's an awesome and integral part of who I am. Making and sharing food with my family is a significant event, not just on holidays but every day. My family's history, along with my collection of experiences around them, has helped to shape who I am today.

But cooking isn't everything. And I reflected on the fact that what we eat is not as important as who we are. As well, it's not just about the food itself: meals bring people together.

As a human being born with unlimited potential, I had to find meaning in other aspects of my family history.

I recognized that one of my greatest gifts is my ability to connect with people, especially children. My great-grandfather was the one who blessed me with this gift in my own childhood. It was the tickling that started it. He was great at making all his grandchildren and great-grandchildren laugh. I remember running over to him at the end of the school day so that he could pick me up and tickle me. This created a connection between us.

When my own grandsons were toddlers, I started to take them to the hockey rink. Some days, my neighbour Dennis would come to help out, but Dennis didn't skate. I was on the ice with them, and Dennis would sit on the sidelines assisting the kids with their runny noses and skate laces.

"Karl, I would love to be the kind of everyday grandfather you are," Dennis would say to me. Dennis did have a grandson, but he lived in Oshawa, not right around the corner like mine, and so he missed many of the moments I enjoyed.

Just then, I picked up one of the boys, calm as anything.

"See," Dennis said, "when I pick up my grandson, he's wiggling, he's punching, he's screaming to be put down! My relationship with my grandson is not like your relationship with your grandchildren."

"Well, Dennis, if you want to connect with little kids," I said, "I have two simple rules to offer you."

"What are they?"

"Never look them in the eye. That's rule number one. Because if I'm not around them all of the time, they don't know me. There's something about looking them in the eye that bothers a child. Pick them up and face them outward."

"Okay, good rule."

"And then, second, play with their tummy. Tickle them and they'll love it. Make them laugh."

"Geez, you know what? I'm gonna try that."

Imagine my surprise when Dennis showed up the next week and told me that he tried out my two simple rules.

"I went out on a date yesterday," Dennis said. "And I tried your method."

"My method? What do you mean?"

"Well, I never looked her in the eyes. And I tried to tickle her tummy. And it didn't work! She never returned my call."

I couldn't help but laugh out loud. But Dennis's misunderstanding of my story also made me rethink my advice.

Our deep roots not only hold messages for us, they form a foundation for self-understanding. My method of forging connections with my family, tummy tickles and all, wouldn't necessarily work for Dennis, but it had meaning for me.

We all have stories from our pasts that are meaningful to us. But the difference between stories and myths is important.

Every family has a set of stories that define them, their norms and values, and their ideas of what it means to meet their potential. Life experiences provide important stories that exist to anchor us.

For example, there was and is a direct line between my great-grandparents' way of life, my father's decision to move from Jamaica to start over in Canada, my life, and the lives of my children. Everyone in my family did what they had to do to make sure we had a happy and secure family home. In our case, that meant we felt comfortable with taking chances. My father ended up moving all of us to Sudbury, where he was able to get a good job working as a diesel mechanic at Falconbridge. Our lives could have easily taken a different path, because it was difficult for my parents to come to a new country with three young boys and begin a whole new life, but they were brave enough to do so. I took a similar chance and moved my own family to Toronto in order to ensure that my children would be able to compete in sports at the highest possible level. Today, my children are following the same path with their lives, taking calculated risks to reach their potential.

These are our family stories: They are the true-life experiences that define us. They are part of the culture of us, and we tell them over and over again.

Life experiences provide important stories that exist to anchor us.

What is a myth, and what does it have to do with our roots?

Myths are different than stories. Myths connect our stories to social understandings, but they are also, for the most part, false. *Myths make your root system weak.*

Myths evade the truth. When we try to find an easy explanation for something complex or nuanced, we create a box around a story to make it fit. Anything that you say, out loud or to yourself, that starts with "I'm too," "I always," "I will never," "My family doesn't," is more likely to be a myth than a story.

Stories can sometimes fuel the myths we tell ourselves about ourselves. For example, instead of thinking that my father was brave for coming to Canada, what if we had thought that he was foolish for leaving his island home? Would that have fuelled our potential? Or would that have diminished it? How would we have felt about who we are as a family? How would it have affected my siblings when it came to thinking about their own potential? How would it have affected me?

Myths can also go the other way around. Sometimes, we grow up believing that we have to be, act, or thrive in a certain way if we are going to be successful. That myth can leave us feeling dejected, disappointed, and shamed if we don't live up to those expectations.

For example, I read about a professional boxer who was chasing a single dream. His dream was to be the heavyweight champion of the world. He won an Olympic gold medal in boxing along the way, and then, after stepping in the ring for his championship fight for the heavyweight title, he stepped out of the ring wearing the belt. His primary reason for fighting was to win the championship. His primary purpose for living was to win the belt.

But because the myth he was holding in his mind was that winning that title would solve all of his problems, his boxing career ended when he reached his destination.

He stopped fighting.

He stopped thinking.

He stopped working.

He stopped living.

There was no dream for him to chase.

Eventually, his life fell apart. His money was all gone, along with his friends, who were hanging onto his fame. He was no longer a famous boxer. He became famous for losing it all. His best life had been when his boxing dream was at arm's length, when he was expecting to feel fulfilled. When that feeling didn't happen, he lost all hope. That's why, sometime after his boxing life ended, this accomplished man had to begin his most important fight, namely the fight to save his life.

What happens when we mix up our stories and our myths?

To reach your maximum potential, you may want to follow the ways of the ostrich.

Ostriches are very large birds; perhaps, if you've never seen one before, larger than you imagine. Males can reach almost ten feet tall. That's a height that exceeds that of the average living room.

You'd think that, being so tall, ostriches would be able to stand up to anything and anyone. Often, they do. They can fight. If cornered, an ostrich can deliver a kick capable of killing a lion. That's twice as powerful as the best boxers, and, even more frightening, they have sharp talons at the ends of their feet.

We've all heard the common story about ostriches burying their heads in the sand, though, so what's the real story? Are ostriches really problem avoiders? Or are they fighters? We've mixed up a myth about ostriches with the authentic reason why they exhibit this behaviour. And it's a valuable behaviour.

As flightless birds, ostriches don't build nests in trees. Instead, they dig holes in the sand and lay their eggs there in order to keep them safe from predators. To make sure that the eggs are warm and in good shape, they occasionally displace the sand around the nest and stick their heads inside to rotate the eggs. From afar, it looks like a caring parental ostrich is trying to hide. But let's face it, if an ostrich was up against a lion, they wouldn't last long with their head underground.

Stories can hold both deep meaning and deep wisdom, and so can myths. If everything we experience is a story, who is the author? What do you actually believe?

Too often in life we are striving for that mythological future, for better, for what we don't have and what we didn't get when we were growing up, rather than looking at all the options that are available to us in life. When we do this, we can lose sight of our roots and the foundational experiences that shaped us into the people we are and that provide us with the buffering support we need when we fall. And we will always fall! And we may lose our own stories of our life, of our ancestors, and of the experiences we share in our communities. Because let's face it: difficult times will continue. Obstacles will come up and try to block us from reaching our destiny. But when we know who we are and how we overcome our challenges, we can get ourselves on the path to being resilient.

Think about this deeply. As children we came into this world with a personality, but not with a true identity. Our identity is crafted for us by our parents, our community, and our own experiences. At some point, we buy into that identity. Eventually, our identity begins to evolve. We start to understand our family stories, and we may even create myths around our own experiences to help us sort out where we fit in, and where we do not fit in.

Myths can be very helpful or insightful and even great fun. They can also be unconscious blockers that hamper our self-awareness, potential for growth, and they may ultimately cultivate our fears. Myths are downright powerful as they have a subliminal quality to them that can inform our subconscious mind in profound and deep ways. If we believe myths, then that perspective may be running the show. Ultimately, being aware of our collective and individual mythology is not just helpful, it's critical to our understanding of ourselves, our community, our behaviours, and even our world as a whole.

When you know your goals and dreams, you need to take the necessary steps to reach your maximum potential.

You have to pay attention to what you have in your nest.

You have to measure yourself.

You've got to observe yourself.

You can't be afraid of what's going to break open, right before your eyes.

You have to nurture what you want to create in your life.

Believing: Your Root System

Who can write the stories of our past, our present, and our future?

You can!

You can turn your personal stories into powerful allies! You can create a set of stories of the most awesome version of yourself that you could possibly imagine. You can develop stories that support a forward-looking and aspirational version of yourself. You can build a story of your actual potential.

Remember, our life stories and our myths start in our root systems. We all have the potential to be winning and beautiful and loving and brilliant! But we also have to acknowledge that stories about our identities can become ingrained over time, and these can shift into myths.

Roots keep you grounded. That's why it's critical to connect our roots to our present-day experiences and values rather than to the myths that bind us.

Answer these questions.

▶ What stories from your personal history speak to your heart, your inner spirit?
▶ What myths that you learned to believe about your past self are holding you up right now?
▶ What stories are keeping you from blowing away in the storm?
▶ What myths do you want to eliminate from your life?

Finding your roots is also about discovering the depth of the relationships and experiences that you chose to have in life, so that you can build new, better foundational stories to support your growth.

The people I have connected with the most in my own life are those who make it a priority to move past the superficial in conversation. We allow ourselves to share our important stories. Instead of being guarded, we take down our masks together. The depth of these relationships makes all the difference in the quality of my daily life, because it allows me to talk through situations with people who share my values and concerns. When we are able to break through that suit of armour, we can get to the core of our goals and dreams.

Your roots take shape from wherever your seeds are planted.

Our stories emerge from our upbringing, our culture, our values:

▶ Our roots begin to grow when we understand where we are from geographically, culturally, and socially.

▶ Our roots may include stories told to us by our parents and grandparents, but not always! Some of our most important stories emerge from our own experiences with our best friends, teachers, coaches, and spiritual guides.

▶ Our roots can include the foods we cook, the languages we speak, and the traditions we share.

Our stories can also emerge from seeds we plant ourselves:

▶ Our stories can be an amalgamation of who we have become over time and the aspects of ourselves that we know we can count upon.

▶ Our stories can include our core accomplishments and an understanding of who we are as individuals.

▶ Our stories can include things we know about ourselves, the deepest part of ourselves.

The important part is that your story begins where you want it to begin. As a story unfolds and is retold, it can become a clearer message to yourself as well as to others. Stories connect people because each one of us has stories. Your roots are not just your physical origin, but the origin for the potential you are in the process of capturing. The stories we create right now are what provides us with power. Regardless of our vision and goals, which may be ever-changing, we need our roots to thrive.

Understanding yourself fully means that you have to take stock of where you come from and what impact you want to have on the world. Honour your past and your people, and trust in your instincts about who you want to become.

To do this, we can name the aspects of our chosen life story that are the most important to our growth.

Exercise Your Potential: Your Core Self

To root yourself, I want you to choose a word or phrase that represents your current story.

Words are powerful allies. Words are the roots of stories. Your root word or phrase will be an affirmation that reflects your core self. This word will help you motivate and inspire yourself to reach your potential.

1. Make a list of your top three accomplishments from this past year. Explain how you made each of them happen. Then write down a single statement about the underlying belief or life experience that allowed you to achieve that success.

2. Make a list of areas in your life in which you did not accomplish all you had hoped to within the last year. Also list what you now know you could have done to achieve successful outcomes.

3. Choose the single most positive, powerful, and simple statement, based on these lists, that will energize you and help you focus when you need it the most. It could be one word or a few words that describe what you want to achieve. If it is a phrase, it should be stated as a positive statement in the present tense, like "I am authentic and true in all things that I do."

4. Bring this word or phrase to mind any time you need to be reminded of your powerful focus and belief in your ability.

5. Say your word or phrase out loud to yourself, in the mirror, in the car, taking a walk.

Remember, no one can have or share your true-life story. It's not possible.

You are unique, as is your story, and you are allowed to write it yourself.

PART IV

THE
DOING
YOU

CHAPTER 13

What Is Doing?

While visiting my family in my home country of Jamaica, I decided to go to a beautiful botanical garden in Montego Bay. I was fascinated by the variety of plants, and by all of nature's gifts.

Before I took the tour that day, I didn't know many of the species of plants native to Jamaica, even though I had lived there as a child. I know a mango tree when I see it. I know a coconut tree, of course.

But when the tour guide stopped at one particular tree to tell us about it, I was confused.

The tree was no longer alive.

Some of its branches were hardened by the weather. The rain and sun had taken their toll. It looked fundamentally fossilized. It was good firewood, if anything.

"Look at this!" the guide said, pointing to it. "This is the No-Problem Tree."

I started to laugh. In Jamaica, "no problem" is a phrase used in conversation all the time.

"Why is it the No-Problem Tree?" I asked him.

"Well, sir, since it died, it is no longer a problem for us. We don't have to do anything to take care of it anymore!"

He was right. The No-Problem Tree wasn't a problem because no one was watering it. No one was feeding it. Once, it was alive and growing branches and leaves and maybe fruits. It fed the birds and the animals of the forest around it. It had great value. But now, no sunlight was required to help it grow because it simply wasn't growing at all. Perhaps it had suffered a little in the weather, perhaps it had been affected by disease. But no matter what, the tree wasn't a problem any longer.

The No-Problem Tree was like a no-problem dream. If you don't take action to feed, water, and care for your dream, it'll end up the same way: fossilized.

You might think to yourself, isn't a dead dream an actual problem? It can be. A no-problem dream might serve a purpose just as a living dream does, but that purpose is different. The purpose of a no-problem dream is to remind us that action is a major part of reaching our potential. If we're not watering a tree, we're not seeing it reach its potential as a core part of an ecosystem. Similarly, if we're not living our dreams, we're not living the life we were made to live.

I'm beginning this chapter with a story about failure precisely because that's what we are afraid of the most.

We're afraid of the problems ahead of us, the ones that we'll create if we don't do everything right, and in the right order. Often, when our dreams don't come to us easily, we blame ourselves for failing to achieve our goals. We have this feeling that failure is final. As soon as we fail, it's done. We're finished. There's no more.

But that's not really true. If a dream withers, you can start growing another one.

Failure is a place where we learn to change direction. Failure prompts us into taking action. Failure is the place from which we learn and we grow and we get better. Of course, we want to make our dreams a reality and follow a path of least resistance. We want to follow our passions because we want to be happy. We want to have success as we ourselves define it.

Unlike the No-Problem Tree, our dreams not only need to grow, they need to branch out. They need to drop their seeds into the soil. The more you dream, the more branches you create. And the longer those branches are, the greater your impact and the more success you'll be able to reach.

Are you a human being, or a human doing? When I speak to my students, I don't ask them *what* they want to be when they graduate from school.

Instead, I ask them *who* they want to be.

"Mr. Subban, I want to be a doctor when I grow up" is something I hear all the time.

"That's good. I believe in you," I say. "So what are you doing today to support that dream? What kind of person are you today, right now? Why are you in school?"

"I don't know," one student answered. "I come to school to learn, I think."

I know it's a hard question for a kid to answer, especially a kid whose parents only have a high school education and never went to university to become doctors themselves. But it became clear to me that some of my students did not know why they came to school. I wanted them to be able to discover who they were inside and what matters to them, before anything else.

Are you a human being, or a human doing?

"A dream isn't a helium balloon that we have to run and catch as it floats further and further away. The balloon is something that we actually have to tie down before we inflate it. I look at your report cards right now, and I don't see a lot of evidence of learning there," I responded to my student. "I look at your notebook. I don't see a lot of evidence there. Right. I look at your test scores. I don't see a lot of evidence there. Not yet! But you can get there."

"I don't know what to do, though."

"Let me give you a reason why you are in school, and you can use it until you come up with a better one of your own. Repeat after me: I come to school to work hard to be a better person, a better student, and a better athlete."

I make my students memorize that mantra, and when I stop them in the hallway to ask how they are doing, they're able to say it loud and proud.

In the kinds of inner-city schools I've worked in, I'm never looking for any of my students to get an A+ on every test or score the most goals in the big game. What I am looking for is students who show me that they are working, period.

Why? Because actions are where potential transforms into power.

Doing: The Four-T Method

You can't force yourself into raising your own roof. You have to *want* to take action in order to make action.

There are four steps that my students follow to take action and to become more successful on their own terms than they ever dreamed possible. I call it the Four-T Method.

1. Time

The first step is understanding and using time to our personal advantage. In the world we live in, timing is everything. We have to not only show up on time, we have to make time to do the things we love and value. We give time to our friends and family. We get frustrated with the amount of time we have to spend on tasks that aggravate us, like driving in traffic and doing our taxes.

So, I'm asking you to be punctual and complete tasks on time, just like I expect from my students.

It may sound old-fashioned, but being truly punctual means that you have the ability to complete a task or fulfill an obligation before or at a designated time. Punctuality is valuable for you in that it helps you keep track of what you have to do and when. It's also valuable for others, in that being on time is a sign of respect and professionalism. Punctuality means that you're organized, committed, and dependable.

Take a look at your schedule, daily or weekly, and create a new, potential-focused version of what you have to do and when. My recommendation is to work on paper. As a teacher, I know that it makes a big difference when we can be creative on the page. Writing and reading our handiwork can help us remember what is important to us.

There are lots of wonderful punctuality tools out there to help you, like:

- a bullet journal, following Ryder Carroll's method, which offers a way to use any notebook to create a customizable planner that is specific to your needs
- traditional planning systems like those from Blue Sky, MochiThings, Panda, and Hobonichi
- planners for people with executive functioning challenges such as ADHD, including Seeing My Time and Happy Planner

2. Task

Of course, knowing what tasks you need to accomplish in order to master your craft is a major component of taking action.

That may be a given, but what I have also learned in life is that doing something for doing's sake equals doing nothing. That's because if the tasks you have assigned yourself are sapping your energy, then they aren't worth doing at all. You need to decide what tasks are likely to feed your goals and what tasks are just window dressing.

For example, perhaps you want to start a new business. Tasks that are going to move the needle include making a strategic plan, figuring out a budget, and finding your first customers. Tasks that feel like window dressing might include putting up social media posts before you have any products or services to sell, or buying new computers for employees you haven't hired yet. Deciding which tasks to prioritize is going to make all the difference in reaching your goals right out of the gate.

Think about the kind of things you like to do, tasks that feel energizing rather than draining.

How does each of your tasks connect to your purpose?

What order should you put your tasks in?

Which of those tasks do you feel are allowing you to reach your potential? Which are not?

What tasks are you missing?

Can you do all of these required tasks to the best of your abilities?

If not, what is stopping you? Do you need more information? More tools and resources? Help from a friend or colleague?

Once you are able to answer these questions, connect your tasks to your schedule. Make sure you include tasks that keep you going on a personal level. Your passion is important, and you're allowed to want and work towards a beautiful future that includes daily tasks that do nothing other than make you happy.

3. Train

Training is about taking the time to continually repeat your skills in order to improve your outcomes.

In sports terms, it's pretty easy to define training. You practise! But what most people don't realize is that it's the same thing for other goals. Practice makes progress no matter what you're trying to achieve in life.

"It's not that I'm so smart," Albert Einstein once said. "It's just that I stay with problems longer."

He wasn't wrong. Einstein excelled at physics and mathematics from an early age, but he found it difficult to get into a post-secondary education program because he was too focused on his subject area and didn't have a well-rounded skill set. For many years, he was a clerk at the Swiss patent office. Einstein didn't get a job teaching at a university until he was thirty years old. But even while he was working in an administrative role, he kept on practising his skill set in physics. Einstein even published four academic treatises, including the one we've all heard of detailing his ground-breaking theory of relativity, while he was pushing papers and red tape every Monday to Friday.

A lot of times, we give up too easily. We're going to face problems that will distract us emotionally. We're going to face barriers that can distract us physically. Distractions compel us to go the wrong way on a one-way street. They may even cause us to get into an accident. And we're not going to reach our destination if we let accidents get in our way. Eventually, we have to leave that accident scene.

That's why, when things are tough, our only choice is to train more.

What do you need to train yourself on? I'm not talking about your tasks; I'm talking about the things you need to practise to become exceptional as a person.

Don't just think about the big things. Sure, a hockey player needs to be able to skate and pass well. But they also need to have communication skills, great timing, and endurance. Business leaders don't just need to learn how to create strategies. They also need to be able to listen well in the workplace. Teachers need more than public speaking practice and a set of textbooks. They also need to comfort a crying child and act as a bridge between parents and administrators.

What are the big and small things you need to practise? How often do you need to practise them? Can you practise them every day? If not, why not?

Falling in love with the process is critical, because doing takes practice. The only thing better than practising seven times a week is practising eight times a week.

4. Team

Co-operating with others to achieve better results is an essential part of every person's action plan. Everyone needs a team to help them reach their potential. I don't mean a sports team. I mean the team of people you surround yourself with day to day.

One night, I went for dinner at a fabulous restaurant, and because the meal was so outstanding, I asked to meet the person in charge of the cooking.

"How did you become a chef? How did you become the person you are today?" I asked him when he came out of the kitchen.

"Karl, I always wanted to be a chef," he said, shaking my hand. "But my father didn't see the chef in me. He wanted me to be a mechanical engineer. So you know what I did? I went to engineering school, and the day I graduated and they gave me my diploma, I returned home as quickly as I could. I handed the diploma to my father, and said, 'Here, this is for you.'"

Co-operating with others doesn't mean following their dreams.

It means that you have to surround yourself with people who understand *your* dreams and who are going to support you and help you when the going gets tough.

There is research now telling us that we are very much impacted, motivated, and driven by our environment. And, according to motivational speaker Jim Rohn, the five people you spend the most time with shape who you are.

Look around you right now. What do you notice when you think about the people you are spending your time with? You may interact with many individuals every day, but there are also those people in your life who are always around: your family at home, your colleagues at work, your fellow students in your community classes, the friends you meet daily at your favourite coffee shop. How do they impact your thinking and decision-making? How do they elevate or drown out your thinking and personal performance? What changes do they bring about in your life? Are these changes positive or negative?

That's why your job is not necessarily to join a team, but to discover your team.

Who do you know right now who gives you hope in reaching your potential?

Who holds out their hand to lift you up when you falter?

Who has their own dreams that parallel yours and is also willing to follow the Four-T Method to take action on their future?

Think about how you can connect with your team and how you can energize each other into taking your next best steps together. Uplift each other. As Martin Luther King Jr. once said, "No work is insignificant. All labour that uplifts humanity has dignity and importance and should be undertaken with painstaking excellence."[1]

Exercise Your Potential: Branching Out

How will you branch out into the world?

There are a lot of different ways to take action, depending on your dreams, your goals, and your purpose in life.

Action plans are often like to-do lists. They connect the dots between what you want to do and what you have to do to get to your end goal. Any business plan can be an action plan, especially if you are borrowing money from a bank or a business partner. Taking a university degree usually follows an action plan, especially if you have a specific career objective in mind.

But taking action doesn't necessarily mean that you have to create a strategic plan and follow it through step by step right away.

In fact, before you decide what you are actually going to do, we need to talk about the kinds of actions that you actually *enjoy* doing on a day-to-day basis.

Which of the following action sets are oriented to your dreams, ideas, talents, and skills? You don't have to choose just one. In fact, I'd like you to choose your top three. Write down how you'd apply at least one of these action sets to the dream at the top of your dream tree.

- ▶ **Reach and balance.** You know you want to get things right, but not just for the sake of being right. You want to engage others in being ethical and applying high standards in their lives so that we all have the best of ourselves in our world.
- ▶ **Comfort and calm.** You are focused on your internal experience and those of others. You are wonderful at expressing yourself so people will understand that they are healthy and see themselves as unique and special. You want to share your positive internal experience with other people.

- **Source and solve.** You notice what is working and what might go wrong, forecasting problems before they happen so you can prepare for them ahead of time. You are an insightful problem solver and a good troubleshooter, and you know where all the resources are. You want to help make life a little bit easier for other people.

- **Innovate and charge.** You are the best at bringing forth new ideas and planning for the future. You are optimistic, enthusiastic, and automatically reframe negatives into positives. You like creating new options for old challenges, so that people around you feel a sense of excitement about what's possible.

- **Harmonize and bridge.** You bring people together. You are a natural mediator who wants to make sure everyone is heard and different points of view are considered. You know what's necessary to connect stakeholders, and you explore all of the options open to your community or professional group.

- **Light and fire.** You know that people intrinsically understand what matters to them as individuals. You also know that people sometimes lack the ability to see what steps they need to take first. You can provide a foundation for others to move towards the lightest and brightest version of themselves.

To raise your roof, you need to bring awareness to the way you like to operate in the world so that you can take advantage of the gifts you already have in front of you.

Think about these questions as you dream about what you would love to be doing each week.

What does taking action look and feel like?

Who are you doing these things with?

What don't you want to do?

What actions do you want to take first, and why?

Finally, write your own mission statement.

A sailboat without a keel and rudder will be blown wherever the winds and tides direct. In the same way, if you don't have a stated purpose, the winds of life can easily blow you where they will.

Now that you've spent time thinking about what it feels like to take action, spend time developing your vision statement.

An effective vision statement is short and direct. It is the rudder of the vessel, keeping it on track both in challenging and in successful times. Similarly, creating a personal vision statement can give your life new meaning and keep you from falling into familiar patterns or habits. By asking myself the above questions many years ago, I developed my personal vision statement, which is "Whatever you're facing should never become bigger than the dream you're chasing." This vision statement has often helped me to focus on my potential and to understand what is at stake every day that I parent, teach, and coach. There is nothing dazzling about my vision statement any more than there is about a keel hidden beneath a boat, providing stability in turbulent seas.

To start, write a few summary sentences that embody all you have noted down about your action sets.

Then, hone it down. Make it rhyme. Make it fun to remember and to act upon.

Write it down on several index cards and put them in places where you will see them often. For a while, remind yourself every hour of what your vision statement is.

Having a vision statement for your life is a quick and essential way to bring your existence into focus and give you purpose.

CHAPTER 14

Love the Game

"You've got to step up and play, man. You can't worry about criticism. You can't worry about failure. You really can't worry about that stuff. You've got to go out and figure that out and play and do the best you can, and whatever happens, happens. You can't be held captive by the fear of failure or the fear of what people may say."

I listened to Kobe Bryant say those words back in 2014 as he was interviewed on ESPN.[1] My whole life, I had spent a lot of time tuning into sports broadcasts. But in 2014, PK was having one of the best seasons of his career, and sports news was always on in the background.

As I sat down to listen in, I remember the interviewer noting something important. Bryant, as you probably know, was one of the greatest basketball players to ever play the game. Playing with the Los Angeles Lakers, Kobe ranked third in career NBA scoring in all of history. He's also won five NBA championships and two Olympic gold medals, and he has been an eighteen-time NBA All-Star over the course of a twenty-year history in the sport.

But Bryant also has another best-of in the NBA: the most misses.

In his 2018 book, *The Mamba Mentality*,[2] Bryant wrote that his ability to score on the court was only a small part of why he was successful.

Yes, he practised so that he had an incredibly accurate shooting technique.

Yes, he loved collaborating with his teammates.

Yes, he sacrificed time, money, and other aspects of his life to remain dedicated to the game.

But what actually set Bryant apart, in his opinion, was that he never compromised when it came to his attitude.

And there is the difference between this basketball player and many others. Kobe made a choice to never lose his love for the game, and he didn't believe in failure.

When we start to live up to our potential, we often reach a plateau. But if we want to keep growing, we have to remember that we are living, breathing, and coaching ourselves to reach our potential every day. Our potential is infinite. Every day is an opportunity to refine what we want out of life. But we are also learning every single day, and that means we have to be open to changing our dreams as we evolve as human beings.

Raising your roof isn't about just moving forward, it is about understanding and revealing who you really are and what you want to continue to do in your day-to-day life so that you can keep on loving the game you are playing.

Loving the game is a big part of raising your roof.

Once you have mastered dreaming, believing, and doing, the next step is not about just doing the same thing over and over again.

It's about loving what you do so you can aim for more of just that.

The more we try different things along our pathway in life,

- the more we learn what works for us, rather than what we assume works for everyone,
- the more we discover what doesn't work at all,
- the more we find out what we might be good at and uncover new things about ourselves, and
- the more we know what we actually want to spend time doing.

Doing: Build a Forest of Dreams

As Lao Tsu, a contemporary of Confucius, once said, "If you do not change direction, you will end up where you are going."

In order to keep loving what you're doing, you have to set the bar higher than you think you can reach. To reach your potential, you have to keep on reaching, especially if you want to feel good about what you are trying to achieve every day.

But feeling good is sometimes difficult when you're just getting started on your action plan. Your dream tree might feel a little wobbly.

Trees can move as the wind blows. But if your dream tree is caught in a sudden storm, it needs its balance to remain rooted.

You can have a whole forest of dream trees. None of us can live with a single tree in our forest. The size of your dream doesn't matter, and one size does not fit all. My dream is not like your dream. In a forest of dreams, the tallest tree may be your most important dream, but there may be fifty trees in that forest, all waiting for your attention. Why is a forest of dreams important?

1. If you don't dream, you'll never know or learn what you're capable of doing.
2. It is through your dreams that you learn who you really are.
3. You will always conceive of more dreams than you will achieve in your lifetime, and that's a good thing.

But in order to see the forest for the trees, sometimes it helps to write down the goals that you want to achieve. In fact, you don't have to write down just one goal. You can write down many connected goals in order to nurture your dream tree and grow your dream forest.

Get SMART, the Karl Subban way

Over forty years ago, a management consultant from Washington state named George Doran came up with the SMART acronym for goal setting.[3] George ran a small business in the western part of the state, and he helped other small businesses get going. He noticed that many of his clients had fantastic dreams, but few of them were actually achieving them. So he came up with an easy system to help them to narrow down their next steps. His SMART system stands for *specific, measurable, attainable, relevant,* and *time-bound.* It worked.

You may have heard of SMART goals before, but you may not know that this process isn't just effective for businesses. Hospitals use these goals, and so do sports organizations, musicians, authors, and schools, as well as many others. I teach all my students how to use SMART goals. Even small children can conceptualize this process and get excited about what they are going to do next. That's because writing down your SMART goals will break down the doing part into a number of easy-to-follow steps.

So here's my spin on SMART goals.

▶ **Specific.** George wrote about setting a specific target area for improvement as a first step. I agree! This is probably the hardest part of designing a goal for yourself, though, and it requires some thinking through. That's why, in my coaching work, I always say that the more specific you can get about your goals, the better.

▶ **Measurable.** You have to be able to see how far you've come to understand where you're going to go next, so you need to measure your progress. To do this, George suggests that you have to be able to quantify your movement forward, which means that he'd like you to put numbers to your practice. In other words, George wants you to measure how fast you're going, how many widgets you're making, and how long you work in a day. Those are all great things for businesses. But when it comes to our personal goals, how we feel is just as important as how many check marks we have on our to-do list.

▶ **Attainable.** When George originally wrote up his concept of SMART goals, the A stood for *assignable*. He wanted his clients to decide who on their team would act on their collective plan. Since this book is about reaching your own potential, the person doing the work is always going to be you. When we're devising SMART goals, we have the ability to climb each rung up to our highest bar. In Kobe's balance between loving the game and constant self-improvement, he knew when to set a number of attainable goals in a row to keep his eye on the long term.

▶ **Relevant.** Your SMART goal has to be relevant to your overall goal. Do you remember that one of the trees in your dream tree is the tallest?

▶ **Time-bound.** You should be able to complete each SMART goal in a set amount of time. Remember how I told you that SMART goals are about breaking down your doing into parts? That's why this kind of goal has to be concrete, not open-ended. You're not solving your whole life's challenges in one fell swoop. Instead, you're making decisions on what you can spend time doing right now to raise your roof. Being open to setting micro-sized goals makes it easier to love the game.

I never want to see my students or coaching clients get bored or fed up on their path forward. But there is another piece of wisdom that I need to pass on to you: you're allowed to discern what you love about your dream, and you're also allowed to discern what you can or want to alter or discard about your dream along the way.

Climbing El Capitan, a vertical rock formation in Yosemite National Park, takes a significant amount of physical and emotional courage. It takes an expert four days to achieve this goal, even after years of training.

The courage that it would take me to do the same thing, walking into that park today and being handed some equipment I've never used before, is likely more than that of a rock-climbing expert, however.

Why? Because the expert has skills. The expert already knows what to do. Her brain has different wiring. She doesn't have the same fear of heights that I would have at the top of a very tall mountain. She knows that environment, so she's not sensitive to the concerns that would rack my brain. That's just reality.

What lesson can we learn from observing the difference between the expert and me? It's that what defines us is our experiences in life.

Courage is subjective. It might be courageous to climb a mountain. It may also be courageous to walk around the mountain. It can even be courageous to just walk outside of your own home. We can't even imagine how much courage it takes certain people to achieve certain things. It takes courage to be awake. It takes courage to be intentional with our life.

Being open to setting micro-sized goals makes it easier to love the game.

That's why, when we are giving ourselves the chance to reach our potential, it has to be okay to set goals, and it also has to be okay to say, "Not today." It takes courage to admit that we are not ready right now. It takes courage to ask, "If not today, then when?"

That's where our SMART goals come in. We have the ability to pick and choose what gives us joy on our path so that we can love the game every single day. We can even decide on a few different goals we can follow over the course of a few weeks, weaving between them depending on what we have the energy for each day. Because practice is a big part of nurturing our dream tree, we can focus that practice on what makes sense to us, as long as we have a specific, measurable, attainable, relevant, and time-bound set of actions in mind.

Exercise Your Potential: Write SMART

Now, I want you to write down your first SMART goal. In fact, you can write down three goals if you want to. Remember, you want to raise your roof! You can blow the roof right off the top of your house with your SMART goals.

▶ **Specific:** Don't make your one and only goal winning the Stanley Cup. Make your goal to practise how to turn on a dime on the ice, or to understand which plays are the most effective in a crunch.

▶ **Measurable:** Think about both quantitative and qualitative measurements, so that you can understand what you do and also whether your plan feels like it's working for you.

▶ **Attainable:** Think about the attainability of your goal. Now, I want you to be very careful in how you interpret this ask. I'm not asking you to lower your expectations. In fact, I want you to do the opposite. Vet your goal to see if it's something you can do or practise with your current skills and resources. If it's not, you may need to reach out for help, or make your goal more specific and attainable so that you can master it on your way up that ladder.

▶ **Relevant:** Think about whether your SMART goal will help that tree grow. If it doesn't, then it may be taking you off track. Make sure that all of the SMART goals you pursue connect back to the potential that you see in yourself.

▶ **Time-bound:** Think about the exact amount of time you want to spend on this goal each day, and when you aim to wrap it up. Write that timeline down. Only you can imagine where and when you might change direction and whether that will take place now or later.

With greater awareness of who you are and what you are loving about your life comes greater responsibility and almost unlimited potential.

This is when we realize that the only rules that exist are those we set for ourselves, and everything becomes even simpler.

There is enough time to reach our potential.

In fact, there is the perfect amount of time.

There's beauty in knowing that we have a whole forest of dreams open before us. We have thousands of choices, and each one of these choices will allow us to move towards our goals. Everything about this process becomes more intentional as our self-awareness increases along with our skills in working towards our potential.

And, when it comes to raising our roof, it is our intentions for ourselves that really matter.

CHAPTER 15

Throw Rocks with Strangers

Walking home along a dark path one night, I couldn't quite see what was ahead of me.

It had been a long day, and a stressful one. There had been some everyday work stress on my plate, but also hockey stress. Throw in some life stress as well. It was just one of those days we all have once in a while, the kind that puts you on edge. It was really good to walk the couple of kilometres home rather than drive. I wanted to blow off some steam and relax, so that by the time I got home, I would be prepared for the kids and ready to start the cycle of a school night all over again.

It wasn't completely dark on the Toronto city path. But I had reached a part of the journey I used to call Snake Alley. I called it that because it was an area covered with thick vegetation, overgrown with trees and bushes, with the path winding through it. Even though it's not far from the road, because of the overgrowth, you can't see many headlights or street lights shining down. You just have to trust that you can make it around the corner from memory.

About twenty feet ahead of me, I thought I saw something. It looked like something crouching on the path, big enough that I could feel my fear grow inside of my chest. I thought I was in danger from a wild animal. I knew I was in the outskirts of the largest city in Canada, but there are still black bears in our midst, as well as coyotes.

I looked around me in the sparse light and thought for a moment. What could I do? A sudden brainwave jolted me into action, and I started to gather all the rocks I could find, just in case. Maybe I'd have to defend myself, or maybe I could just scare the beast off by making some noise. In either case, I started throwing the stones at the shadowy figure in front of me.

Strangely, the figure on the path didn't move. It didn't flinch. And so I kept throwing the stones, standing as still as I could, wondering what might happen next.

Suddenly, a stranger came up from behind me and asked me what was going on. I quickly whispered the story to him, and he started throwing rocks at it, too.

"I can't see it," he said. "I'm going to get a little bit closer."

"No, don't!" I said as he moved a couple of feet down the path.

I held my breath.

He was still moving closer, so I put my hands down in case I hit him with one of the rocks I still held. The fear was building up in me. *This guy is brave*, I said to myself.

"Buddy, I can't help you if you get hurt," I said.

He got so close to it, his feet were almost touching . . . *it*. That's when the stranger took a big sigh of relief.

"It's a pile of rocks," he laughed, turning back to me.

There was no bear, no coyote, no crouching person waiting to pounce. We had been face to face with a mere pile of rocks half hidden in shadows.

I had a deep realization in that moment on the path home from work. Right before I took my first step down that path, I was under the impression that I was a leader. Being a parent, a principal, a coach, I was someone people counted on to help them through challenges, to lift them up. To dry their tears. To stand up for their rights. To fight off the boogeyman in the closet.

But on that path that night, I let someone else step forward. I didn't feel like a leader. I felt scared, almost as if I were a child back in Jamaica and not a very tall and very confident man, ready to take on anything that stood in his way.

Maybe it was because I'd had a bad day, or maybe it was because I was outside of my comfort zone. But I needed to lean on someone else to get through my predicament. This experience raised a number of questions for me to mull over as I got closer and closer to home.

How do we find a balance between looking to ourselves and looking to others to help us on our way to reaching our potential?

How do we discover all the potential we have within us if we feel uncertain?

Should we just keep throwing rocks in the dark?

When I got home, I wrote two contradictory things down:

• It is important not to put our personal burdens onto other people and to recognize our flaws. Knowing we are not alone in our journey is important, but knowing that we also have the ability to take a step forward on our own is a big component of our personal growth. Reaching our potential requires more from us than setting a goal, even if we can dream, believe, and do in an effective way. Reaching our potential requires taking on new responsibilities and thought processes, and it can require a lot of courage. *To do this, we all need self-awareness: an understanding of where we can support ourselves and stand on our own and where we need to build our confidence.*

• Even so, more often than not, when we need each other to reach our potential. We all have to be aware of our environment and our community, and how we can act in defence of each other.

Sometimes spending time with others enhances and builds our potential in ways that we can't achieve on our own. Whatever we're going through right now and whatever challenges we're facing, there are other people who not only understand those challenges but are probably walking down the exact same path. We have to learn exactly how to reach out to those we need beside us in our personal growth journeys. *To do this, we all need other-awareness: an understanding of where we can use our connection with others as a support system and where we can give back to our community.*

Doing: Celebrate Community

Knowing the value of community is essential to reaching your potential. Here are some ways to think about and celebrate community in relation to your goals:

- ▶ Decide to stop wasting valuable time and mental energy being fearful, guilty, angry, and worried, and instead, connect with a friend when you are feeling in need of support.
- ▶ Decide to finally commit to the idea that there is no such thing as a bad situation, there are only learning situations in which you have the ability to build on what others have taught you.
- ▶ Decide to keep in mind that all challenging situations can make you more aware of the value of connection and fellowship, and that all situations have the opportunity within them to give love.

▶ If you want solutions to dissatisfaction and stress, start by asking yourself this: Is my current thinking taking me where I want to go or perpetuating my unhappiness?

The ROCKS method of awareness takes us beyond a growth mindset.

The ROCKS method represents the next phase in reaching our potential because it helps us dig into some of the more complex parts of being human. The ROCKS method balances our growth with our responsibility to the people around us. The acronym ROCKS stands for *relationships, open mind, character, knowledge,* and *service.*

Relationships

There are so many rocks in the path we cannot see. My ability to relate to other people helped me listen to that stranger standing by my side on the dark path. Relationships are important because they help us deal with many of the obstacles we are unable to face up to, or can't see because of our personal blind spots.

Leaders require relationships just as much as they require charisma. There is no possible way to extract the self-awareness of a leader from the performance of a group, community, school, or workplace, because without self-awareness, there is no trust. Sharing what is personal, sharing what is meaningful to each of us allows for aligned growth and awareness of how to build our social relationships. Relationships can bridge any number of life's gaps, because they allow us to overcome obstacles through collective behaviours.

But having good relationships with others is also about self-awareness. When we don't trust ourselves, we remain in bad relationships where we don't trust and are not trusted back, wrecking our self-esteem. We work harder in jobs where we aren't valued and won't ever get ahead, creating layers of physical and mental strain that may never abate. We blame others for our "bad luck" instead of trying something different that may allow us to reach our potential.

Open Mind

An open mind is a gold mine.

We get a lot of our best ideas from creative thinking. And sometimes, that creative thinking isn't what we expect.

For example, let's look at what it takes to climb a mountain.

To get to the top of a mountain like Everest, what do you think is the number-one quality you need? I'm willing to bet that a lot of you would say perseverance. After all, when the going gets tough, the tough get going, correct?

Wrong.

Mountaineers are top performers in making decisions under duress in a group. That much is true. But when American organizational psychology researchers took a look at how mountaineers actually succeeded in getting to the top, they found that too much perseverance made them fail at the task.[1]

In other words, if a group of people continually push each other to their limits, they don't get enough rest. They also keep on hiking when they're injured, leading to more injury as well as mental strain. It's a causal loop that disintegrates relationships and people. Ultimately, perseverance under pressure results in poorer decision-making over the course of a climb. Perhaps even worse, it causes the team to get emotionally off track, meaning that they start to focus on the end result of getting to the top over the day-to-day task of taking the next step on their path.

Elite performers, these researchers explain, know when to stop and take a moment, even several moments or even days. They train themselves to recognize when they, and others in their team, become too desperate to reach a goal, and they simply create another one.

We have to be open to seeing what is actually in front of us, not what we think we *should* be seeing, *should* be doing, *should* be saying. The point of an open mind is to be nimble in every single moment, so that we can adapt to what comes next.

Character

The first Major League Baseball Rookie of the Year Award was won by the late, great Jackie Robinson in 1947. Since then, the Brooklyn/Los Angeles Dodgers have had a record eighteen players take home that prize, twice the number of the New York Yankees, who sit in second place. This includes a streak of five years in a row, when Dodgers players alone were awarded the best rookie awards in baseball each year from 1992 to 1996.

Why?

When sports pundits started looking into their system, they assumed that all of the new players in baseball had major league skills. But the one thing that the Dodgers were able to do was scout the players who had the attitude they needed to make an impact. Instead of just scouting for skills, they scouted for character. That's what separated the players in the Dodgers' lineup from the rest of the league.

Here's what defines character.

▶ Your attitude is positive.
▶ Your work ethic is committed.
▶ You deal with adversity with calmness.

▶ You always act as a role model, even when you are just starting out.

▶ You always take the high road.

Your words become your actions, and your actions become your character, and your character becomes your destiny.

Knowledge

Every seven years, every cell in our body is replaced. Our brains are constantly changing as we grow and learn, building new neural pathways. When we learn ideas or acquire new knowledge, we're developing new perspectives on the world around us.

Psychologists used to think that those of us who managed our lives the best were those who relied on unconscious reactions, what most of us would call a "gut instinct." The reality, though, is that after decades of testing, they found that following our gut instincts actually puts us at a massive disadvantage: we choose the wrong job paths, the most unhealthy foods, and even poor relationships.[2]

The same research has shown that the people who feel more content in life and achieve more of their goals are those who take a bit more of a circuitous path to making a decision. This doesn't mean that they spend a whole lot more time making that decision, but that they have better tools, such as self-awareness, reflection, and adaptability—all skills that are essential in succeeding today and into the future. Developing a conscious-thought advantage still makes use of our tacit, learned knowledge, but it also allows us to play with options in a way that creates new energy around decision-making.

We often don't go deep enough into self-awareness to trust ourselves fully. When I was starting out in life, even though I had an ambition to become the next hockey star, there was something that I truly wanted to do even more. Teaching is not something I wanted to do; I *needed* to do it in order to make the impact I wanted. We should all be acting from a place of confidence and discovery, and a commitment to continuous learning. Life isn't about being the best at something, it is about learning how to adapt to the myriad changes that we will constantly face in every aspect of our existence, every moment we are alive. Perhaps that is what makes us the best at something.

Be intentional about developing your self-awareness as well as your knowledge. Being truly who we are and following our instinctual knowledge means being self-aware about how we bring value to the world, and to our work, and, most importantly, to ourselves.

Service

Muhammad Ali said, "Service to others is the rent you pay for your room here on earth."

We all have the choice about where we can place our energy for ourselves and for others. We can choose to live small or live large. Living large, to me, is living through the lens of unconditional love and being a resource for others.

Service could become a business that you pass along to the next generation. Service can mean that you keep your family stories written and passed along to others so they have an understanding of the past. Service can mean that you teach children music and they carry that with them into adulthood. Service can mean that you care for others' health and you work with them in a way that enhances their lives and well-being. Service can mean that you help develop leaders to become the best versions of themselves. Service is as unique as each one of us is who is reading this book.

Exercise Your Potential: The ROCKS Method

If you don't know the answer to a question, be patient, and sit with "I don't know." If you don't know, remember that you're asking the right questions.

▶ Write down the names of five pivotal people you want to surround yourself with and gain experience and inspiration from. Even if you don't know any people like that by name, describe who they might be. What do they do? Why do you want to get to know them better?

▶ When you think of the term *meaningful relationship*, what does it look like to you? How would you describe a meaningful relationship? What is it based upon?

▶ What are the key characteristics that you desire in your meaningful relationship?

▶ Where can you shift towards building better relationships or finding new ones? What changes can you make in order to move just that little bit further towards trusting those in your community?

▶ When have you had a closed mind in the past?

▶ What could you open yourself up to right now that would help you reach your potential? Think about the limits you have put on yourself before now.

▶ What do you want people to think about you? If you were to receive an award for a great accomplishment, what would it be for?

▶ What questions do you want to ask of yourself, of others, and of the world? If you could take a course right now, what would that course be? Where would you take it?

▶ You may have several ideas of how to serve the world, or you may have none. Find the one that drives you first. Rekindle the passion you may have had to make an impact on others' lives and harness it in a way that is meaningful to you.

In our next chapter, we're going to learn how to shift from planning to follow-through. Together, we'll discover why we're not accomplishing what we think we're supposed to and decide how to actually achieve our dream goals.

CHAPTER 16

Do What You're Doing

Most Toronto neighbourhoods have a soccer field, including the neighbourhood in which I live. During the spring, summer, and fall, children of all ages are there playing soccer, or football as it is known in some places around the world. Soccer players are there chasing the ball, passing the ball, and working and playing to score a goal. The teams show up to score more goals than the opponent and win the game.

There is also something special about the soccer field in my neighbourhood. It isn't just where kids feel at home playing all day, every weekend; it's also the home of the Fruit Man.

The Fruit Man is permanently stationed at the entrance to the soccer park. He shows up when the children are there, evenings, weekends, and holidays, selling a variety of fruits. At one time, I called him the Mango Man because he started out only selling boxes of mangoes.

On the coldest days, the Fruit Man shows up dressed for the weather. On wet days, he is there, too, standing in the bus shelter to protect himself from the elements. The Fruit Man shows up to do his thing day after day, no matter the season or type of weather he is facing.

If he doesn't show up, he won't have any customers.

If he doesn't show up, he won't reach his financial goals.

How do you show up in the different seasons of your life? Not only the meteorological seasons, but the other seasons most people are confronting: seasons of pain, gain, change, and taking charge. To reach your maximum potential, you must learn to show up like the Fruit Man, no matter the season.

The problem is that very few of us are showing up in our own lives. Showing up means that we actually take the time to honour our potential by doing the tasks that get us there.

To help you understand what you need to do, I want to tell you a story about a goat.

At my brother's home in Jamaica, one goat is king. He loves eating not only the grass, but also the newly planted coconut trees. And he knows exactly how to get through the fence when he has his next meal in mind. He follows the dog. My brother's dog is smart and observant, and he found a way to open the gate on his own. The goat clambers through right after him, time and time again.

After replanting those coconut trees too many times, my brother decided to fix the gate so that the dog, and the goat, wouldn't be able to get through it any longer. A childproof lock was installed, and the dog stayed in the yard.

The next day, however, my brother could not believe his eyes: he saw the goat take two steps and then try to hurdle the fence.

The goat didn't make it across. He looked like a plane trying to land, but he skidded into the fence.

Undeterred, the goat decided to lengthen his runway, just like a pilot would. He took a few more steps back, ran at speed, and made the leap.

My brother had to raise the fence.

Sometimes, the goat would go over to the gate and try to use his horns to dislodge it, but eventually, he had to accept the fact that his coconut-tree supply was well and truly out of business.

Looking at the goat, I thought about Serena Williams, the

Greatest of All Time (GOAT) in her sport of tennis. Williams has twenty-three career Grand Slam singles titles, the most of any woman since the open system began. Only Novak Djokovic has bested her record, with one additional title.

Williams had to set realistic goals to win her first title, but after that one, she continued to raise the bar to raise her roof. Just like the Jamaican goat, Williams had to face higher levels of difficulty as she fulfilled her potential. She suffered from health setbacks, and she came back. She gave birth to her first baby, and she came back. She was treated poorly in the media and even by some of her tennis colleagues, and she still showed up to win again.

As we raise our own roof, we may have to make some choices inspired by the goat, or the GOAT.

Think about the amount of time you spend at each task, every day. There are so many demands on your time. The time you spend at work. The time you're with your kids, helping them with their homework or driving them to that soccer field. The time you're doing your taxes and watching television at the same time. The time you're working, driving, and on the phone at the same time because you think you don't have enough time in the day to get things done.

First, we have to stop thinking that we can multitask.

Research shows that in 2023, people checked their phone, on average, once every ten minutes. That's 144 times a day during their waking hours, up from eighty times a day in 2018.[1] In around five years, we've almost doubled the amount of time we spend using our phones to the exclusion of other ways to occupy our minds. In fact, the same research shows that the average person struggles to go more than ten minutes without checking into social media or their email, or playing a game, amounting to four hours and twenty-five minutes each day on their cell phones. People not only do this all day at work, but they can't stop even when they are on vacation.

That means you will spend over two months, namely sixty-five days, on your phone in the next year.

Even so, as author Dave Crenshaw writes in his book *The Myth of Multitasking*, our problem is not just the amount of time we're spending on our phones, it's what happens as a result of doing this all the time.[2] For example, when we pick up our phones to do something quickly while we're already watching television, we lose our sense of rest and relaxation. When we pick up our phones to answer a call while having lunch, we don't digest our food as well. When we pick up our phones to text our spouse while we're in the middle of crunching numbers at work, we lose our train of thought. Doing this over and over again all day negatively affects our bodies and our minds.

> **Think about the amount of time you spend at each task, every day.**

Cutting down on phone use isn't enough to solve the problem, though. Researchers in China, Germany, and the United Kingdom got together to take a look at what happens when we use social media on a near-constant basis.[3] Doing so doesn't simply lead to poor social, academic, and job performance, it also has the potential to decrease our attention spans overall.

How can we get our attention back on our potential?

Are you feeling a sense of mental overload? When I speak about multitasking, does it remind you of patterns in your own life? Here are some clear signs that you might be more distracted than focused:

▶ People close to you often suggest that you slow down and take a break. You don't spend time with friends because you don't have the time to connect.

▶ When you think about working less, you feel anxious. When you think about taking a break, you also feel anxious.

▶ You spend less and less time doing activities that are important to you.

▶ Little, insignificant things start to easily annoy you.

If you're noticing these patterns in your life, it is possible that you've become used to doing too much.

Even when your plate is full, you may continue to take on more tasks. In fact, you may be so used to trying to multitask that when you're not, you feel like something is wrong.

Because you're not wired for multitasking, you may be stressing yourself out by trying to do too many things at once. You may believe that you have no choice other than to do so.

Think again.

The feeling that we need to multitask creates distance between what we want to do with our time and what we actually do. Trying to multitask hampers our ability to think deeply, to focus, and to give attention to what will actually make us feel better and do better in life and at work. Chances are excellent that your to-do list will be a never-ending one, which multitasking won't fix.

If you're always doing something else, when will you dedicate the time to reaching your potential?

If you're always using up your time, when will you be able to grow?

The opposite of multitasking is flow.

Doing: Making Room

There is another way. Not only are *you* more important than your list of things to do, so are the other people in your life. It is easy to put off relating to yourself and your spouse, kids, friends, and animals—but it's better to decide not to. Decide to relate. At least three times every day, take a moment and ask yourself what is really important. Have the wisdom and the courage to build your life around your answer.

I recently came across the following quote that puts priorities in perspective. I don't know where it originated, but its simple wisdom got my attention: "If you knew today was your last day to live, who would you call and what would you say? What are you waiting for?"

We need to make room for new things to happen in our lives if we want to be able to raise our roof.

You can choose to stop living a life where you take on more and feel less.

You can choose to start living a life where you see the importance of balance and where you feel more fulfilled.

The opposite of multitasking is flow. In order to raise our roof, we have to find a balance between routine and free flow, which seems to be one of the greatest challenges that we face. We need to sync our actions to a schedule while simultaneously allowing ourselves the freedom to work from inspiration.

Before we do that, I want to tell you another story about my brother, who has said the following thing to me numerous times:

"The best years of my life, Karl, the best times I've had in my life, were long ago. Those were the days when everyone still lived here. Those were the days my children were right here in my house. They've all moved away. Those were the good days."

I always shake my head.

"I think the best years are still ahead of me," I frequently respond to him. "My best day could even be today."

What's the difference between my brother's point of view and my own?

I believe that if all of my best days are behind me, well, I might as well die right now. What would be the point in living? I'm not advocating for dying, but I am advocating for a change of mindset.

Living in the past isn't going to help you raise your roof.

Living in the past isn't going to make you feel good at all.

In life, we all have a little bit of control over what comes next. We start with the day we are born. We have no control over this day. We end with the day we die. We have little control over this day, either. Unfortunately, we are all going to get there one day. We do have a little bit of influence and control over that, at least some of the time. If we take care of ourselves and exercise and eat well, we may delay the inevitable.

But for the majority of us, the middle our lives is our "window of opportunity." This represents our chance to realize our potential and to live out our dreams.

And so the question then becomes: How are you using your time and energy to reach your maximum potential? Are you relating to people? Are you working through challenges and facing them head-on? How do you want to spend the majority of your life?

The window of opportunity determines how well you live.

We all have that same window. Some people have their windows shut. Their attitude keeps them creeping further away from the possibility of having their best day ever.

But every day has the potential to be your best. Every day YOU have the potential to be your best.

You have control over your window of opportunity. How far are you going to open it today?

The reality is that we do have to make time for open creativity and idea generation if we want to open that window of opportunity.

With creative thinking, the goal is not always clear, and that's why we have to learn to get into flow. The pioneering psychologist Mihaly Csikszentmihalyi has written that flow is a mental state of functioning in which a person is completely immersed in a sense of energy, focus, engagement, and enjoyment of a creative process.[4] Creativity is, in Csikszentmihalyi's point of view, connected to a subconscious force that brings our hidden thoughts and ideas up to the surface. It is up to each of us to give force to those ideas, discovering and sharing something new with the world.

Flow is when we become delightfully lost in the moment rather than focused on our actions.

But to get into flow, we have to make time to do just that.

Let's talk about the science of flow for just a moment.

What allows us to get into flow is known as neuroplasticity. It's the ability of the brain to make new connections between its circuits. We're not actually aware of when this happens because we adjust so quickly that it's barely noticeable. When we're young, our neuroplasticity is what helps our brains develop in the first place. But as we age, we still have the same ability! Our neural circuits can grow and change when we gain access to new information and ideas and learn new habits.

Neuroplasticity is our ability to explore new ideas and learn new things.

Neuroplasticity is the ability of the mind to react to things that happen to us and in the world around us.

Neuroplasticity is how we find new solutions to old problems.

Neuroplasticity is why, as we discussed at the very beginning of this book, it's less important to do something for 10,000 hours. It's better to add to what we know so that we can change for the better over time. That's how we can raise our roof.

Exercise Your Potential: Finding Flow

So let's make it real. How can you find time for your flow?

In seeking time for yourself, you're not seeking something elusive. Time to follow your dreams is always available. Yet it is easy to close the door to personal growth because you believe that something other than raising your roof offers what you want. Creating the time you need to support your commitment to living a more purposeful life is important. This is the stuff from which miracles are made.

Morning: What would your *ideal* morning look like? Write it down.

Evening: What would your *ideal* evening look like? Write it down.

What does the start of a creative endeavour of any kind look like for you? Is there a cup of tea or coffee at your side? Sparkling water? A sunset in the windowscape? Complete quiet or soft noise in the background?

What do you want to feel like when you end your creative process for the day? Will you reward yourself? How so?

What are the feelings you want to nurture in yourself during creative work?

Will those feelings change with the seasons? Narrow your thoughts to creating for the next three months. What does this season look like for you?

What will you say no to so you can allow yourself this mental space and get closer to your ideal morning and night every day?

What will you allow in to break your schedule? You're allowed to stop for meaningful other things. What's most important other than this creative work?

Finally, what are the aspects of yourself that you want to cultivate so you can be the best possible steward of your gifts?

Your goal is to do three things.

1. Spend some time every morning and evening reminding yourself that what you want is to raise your roof and that a daily focus on your own personal growth is central to this. Start with five minutes and work your way up.
2. Spend at least one hour a week planning your next action steps.
3. Once a year, spend a couple of days with a group of people devoted to raising their own roof. Find a retreat or conference that is aligned with your interests, and put it in your calendar.

In the next chapter, we'll look at what happens when we get out of flow and go off course. Don't worry, it happens to everybody! But understanding what to do before you get lost in the forest is a key part of managing course correction with joy and grace.

CHAPTER 17

Taking the Right Course

While on my vacation back home on the sunny island of Jamaica, I went swimming at the local beach, Jackson Bay.

The white sand, manageable waves, hot sun, and sea breeze just slight enough to rock the boat meant that it was a beautiful day. Looking out into the sea was calming, so different from home. The sky above me was almost empty except for the tropical sun and a few birds, pelicans. Some were flying, some were soaring, and some were softly falling into the ocean like Olympic-grade divers jumping off a high cliff.

I saw a single pelican flying above the ocean, surveying the sea for fish. Like a plane preparing to land, it flew barely above the water's surface at times. It would start off in a deep dive, then suddenly abort its mission. Finally, the pelican disappeared under the surface of the water for a few seconds, then reappeared sitting on the water as if it were a boat. I then noticed its long beak and gentle head movement as it swallowed a fish. Mission accomplished. It achieved its goal, but it did not come without work.

To reach your potential, you must work like the pelican, flying, soaring, and diving. Sometimes you must abort your mission. This is when you learn to adapt, adjust, or simply pivot. There is always time to start, or to start over.

The course that you take determines how you get to where you are going.

What do I mean by pivot? To me, a pivot is more than a simple change. It's a recognition that even if we've taken action, that action isn't exactly working for us.

If we want to continue reaching our potential, we must connect with the pelican inside us.

Why? Because if we don't take the right course, we don't grow.

If we aren't feeling like we're moving forward, we literally call it being stuck. And if we don't shift off the path we're on towards something new, we say we're stuck in a rut.

Funny how these terms can mean so much more when they're taken literally!

But we can get unstuck. We can get out of whatever rut we're in. We have to experiment, iterate, and learn, and we have to support investigation, reflection, and creative opportunism. A pivoting mentality allows us to naturally see the opportunities that we already have in front of us every day, creating the space to be curious and authentic about what matters and what is possible for us. And then we have to trust ourselves to act on it.

To move.

To shift.

To grow.

To try.

But what gets in the way of following through and diving into doing? The course that you take determines how you get to where you are going.

Think of your life as a place of education where you have the opportunity to choose what you want to learn. Imagine you can choose between two curricula. One is taught at Fear College; the other at Potential University.

To attend Fear College, the only requirement is to believe that you cannot escape the pain of your past and that you should worry constantly about the future.

To attend Potential University, your only requirement is to believe there just might be a better way to go through life, even if you don't know what it is. No matter what you may have done in the past, you will never be rejected from Potential University.

Take a look at the courses each offers, and decide where you want to learn.

Fear College Course Offerings

▶ **Fear 101: The Use of Guilt and Judgment.** This course teaches numerous ways to beat ourselves (and others) up about things done in the past and about who we believe we are. The premise is that doing this will ensure the student doesn't make any additional mistakes.

▶ **Fear 102: How to Blame the World.** This unique course offers students ways to avoid just about anything. It teaches students that if they don't feel peaceful, all they need do is find something wrong in the external world and blame it. This course is a prerequisite for Avoidance 201: How to Ignore Your Own Responsibility.

▶ **Fear 103: The Ignorance of Time.** Students will learn how to dwell on their own problems and know that trust is a foolish thing. In the second part of the course, students will learn a variety of ways to worry about the future. None of the material teaches students how to work with what is happening at the present time, because, to the fearful mind, the present is dangerous and uncontrollable.

▶ **Fear 104: Desire and Scarcity, the Greatest Motivators.**
Students will be taught that the more they have in this
life and the more they can advertise to others that they are
important, the happier they will be. Scarcity will be taught by
demonstrating that if we give away our time, effort, or love,
we will feel like we have less.

▶ **Fear 105: Control Everything and Be Safe.** The central
teaching of this course is that if we are always right and
everyone else is wrong, we can always be happy. The first part
of the course teaches students that if they can control others,
they will achieve great success. The second part shows how
to use guilt, intimidation, fear, domination, manipulation,
conditional love, and criticism to get what we think we want
out of life.

Potential University Course Offerings

▶ **Potential 101: Self-Acceptance.** This course teaches that the
only thing we can really change is our own mind and our
own action plan. Students are taught to accept what cannot
be changed and change what they can to achieve peace of
mind.

▶ **Potential 102: Understanding Growth.** Learning that there is
no value in holding on to guilt and shame for what we have
or haven't achieved in the past, students discover that every
step they take is the foundation for growth. A dream tree is
accessible to every one of us, and it is up to us to nourish that
tree.

▶ **Potential 103: Change Is Constant.** Students will learn how to discover love by letting go of the past and ceasing to worry about the future. Students remove all limitations from themselves and others by practising the core teaching of knowing that they have permission to change at any point they see fit.

▶ **Potential 104: Abundance.** Students will learn that giving and receiving are equally important. Through ongoing demonstrations, everyone joyfully learns the equation that what is most important—love and compassion—increases as we give it away.

▶ **Potential 105: Sharing Is More than Caring.** Students learn that the greatest source of joy comes from sharing our experiences with others and learning through collaboration and mutual respect. Through service, students learn that assisting others in loving ways gives purpose and meaning to their existence and helps them find new opportunities on their path to growth.

Every minute of every day, you have the ability to make a choice about what you want to learn and what course you want to take.

Both Fear College and Potential University are possible choices, but only one is worthy of your investment. The more you can consciously turn your back on the difficult course load of Fear College and walk towards the growth that is offered by Potential University, the more you will discover the dividends of joy, happiness, and self-acceptance.

You choose your own curriculum. Do you want to be a student of fear or a student of your own potential?

Exercise Your Potential: Getting Unsticky

To get on the right course, unstick yourself.

Imposter syndrome is a very common thing when we are trying to reach our potential. We think that we're not good enough to actually succeed in doing what we want to do. And many of us reject the idea that we can constantly change and shrug off our own potential for development. In fact, we create environments for ourselves in which change is wholly unlikely, because, even if we have a growth mindset, we can slip back into fixed-mindset thinking when we get off course.

So right now, I want you to think very hard about your sticking points. I want you to be very honest with yourself.

1. Do you look to others for approval in order to feel good about yourself?

   Perceived barrier to success: Believing that outside approval is a prerequisite for raising your roof.

   Potential shift: Remember that your potential exists beyond all approval or the lack of it.

2. Do you have a difficult time letting go of frustration in certain situations?

   Perceived barrier to success: Believing that your frustration is always justified and that constantly checking where you are making mistakes will keep you safe.

   Potential shift: Your frustration takes away energy from the time you spend on your own personal growth.

3. Do you believe what others say, even when it results in feelings of shame or ideas of giving up on your dreams?

   Perceived barrier to success: Believing that other people's opinions define who you are and your worthiness for personal growth.

Potential shift: You are forever worthy of reaching your potential. You always have been and always will be.

4. Do you believe that your happiness is dependent on having certain objects or that you need to have a certain look or status in order to reach your potential?

Perceived barrier to success: Believing that how we appear in the world and what we have is the way to attract success into our life.

Potential shift: The potential for our growth is everywhere at all times, independent of anything we have or do not have.

5. Do you look to relationships or work to make yourself feel whole?

Perceived barrier to success: Believing that you are not whole within yourself already and that what you do for work or who you are with is important to reaching your potential.

Potential shift: Your potential is what makes you whole and is within you right now.

6. Do you avoid certain situations because you fear rejection?

Perceived barrier to success: Believing that being a people pleaser and being accepted in all situations by all people is the key to finding your path forward in life.

Potential shift: You are the person who can create connection in your life, and no one can stop you from finding a community to support your personal growth.

7. Do you have a difficult time making decisions and knowing what is right for you? Once you decide something, do you constantly wonder if you made the wrong decision?

Perceived barrier to success: Believing that you can only raise your roof if you always make the right decisions.

Potential shift: Knowing that your decisions don't have to be perfect and that you can pivot any time.

8. Do you feel that things "just happen" to you and that you have few choices in your life? Do you feel that happiness often escapes you?

Perceived barrier to success: Believing that your attitudes and beliefs have little to do with creating the life you want.

Potential shift: Knowing that it is your attitudes and beliefs that either show the path to raising your roof or blind you to it.

9. Do you feel uncomfortable in situations where you are not in control?

Perceived barrier to success: Believing that controlling situations and people is how you make your path to growth sustainable.

Potential shift: Your potential needs no defence or controls; it is always with you.

Now, to unstick yourself, let's look at some of the times when you've been stuck in the past or when you've judged others for their stuckness. Remind yourself that the reason for being stuck wasn't the problem you perceived it to be at the time.

▶ Think about a time when you harshly judged another person for what they had done, but then it turned out they had actually made the right choice for themselves or others.

▶ Think about a time when you have judged yourself as being inferior, less than, dumb, unattractive, or unlovable, but then found out you were able to succeed in doing a difficult task anyway.

▶ Think about a time when you were afraid of something bad happening in the future, but things turned out okay despite your worrying.

▶ Think about a time when you became defensive with someone close to you because you felt embarrassed, but ended up resolving the situation through a productive and mutually kind conversation.

▶ Think about a time when you had to perform at work or school under stressful circumstances, had to give a speech, or had to rush someone to the hospital, and you ended up making sure that everyone and everything was okay.

Reaching your potential to grow always requires practice. Here's the thing.

You're already doing difficult things, and you're already doing great things. In raising your roof, it's your role to build upon these successes.

In fact, in order to reach your potential, you don't have to create something new, take a new course, or change careers.

Take what you are passionate about and make that your focus.

Following your own passion will help you to strengthen your thoughts and ideas further as you delve into your true focus. Daniel Pink describes this type of motivation as evolving from having autonomy, mastery, and purpose.[1] These elements will be critical to motivating you to stay on your path. That is why the more you start where you stand, the further you can raise your roof.

At times, you may feel like you are failing to leave behind anything of significance in your life. I would like to challenge your thinking. This is not failure. It's okay if you're not there yet. It's okay to make a mistake. But it isn't okay to regret the time that you have spent growing. Where we are right now is a result of the decisions and changes we have made in our lives, and that is an amazing thing. Today is a new opportunity to grow again. After all, today is all we have. Right now is all we have. Right now is exactly where we need to be. Right now, we can make a choice to do things differently if we want our lives to be different.

It really is up to us.

Reaching your potential is about your transformation, and so you have to make the choice to transform.

You are learning. You are growing. You are developing a path that is uniquely yours. Use your lived experiences as the foundation to begin to accomplish your goals. Confidence, optimism, and personal experience will help us feel able to seek out information, if and when we need it. In fact, in some ways, you can leave your brilliance behind: you don't have to overthink and overplan everything to get it right. The more you can simplify, the more you can root your ideas into the earth. What you create is not a quick fix; what you create has worth and impact. Reaching your potential may actually be like planting trees whose shade you will not have the chance sit beneath. Yet these trees, the result of your ideas, will have your heart and soul and will continue beyond your time.

Reaching your potential to grow always requires practice.

Why are we so deeply worried about just being ourselves? Why is it so hard to ask for what we want so that we can live our intentions, our intuition, and our ideals?

We have to each be accountable for living our truth in our lives at home and at work. Being truly who we are and following our instinctual knowledge means being self-aware and curious. We have to develop both the curiosity and the opportunity to thrive.

Doing: There Are No Rules

Pretend there are no rules.

What would you really say to someone who hurt you?

To someone whom you admire?

What would you say to yourself about what you need every day to feel comfortable enough to get your work done?

What is the most intimate thing you'd be comfortable sharing now?

What is a simple, positive change that you can offer yourself today?

Don't think about it, just do it.

Like the pelican, take ownership and fly.

When something goes wrong, or when you don't understand what's at stake or even what's happening, check in with yourself first. Be proactively transparent about when you're not perfect. It allows others to be imperfect, too, so that instead of hiding mistakes, we actually own up to them so we can make room for the next step down the path to personal growth.

CHAPTER 18

Start to Finish

An important idea, attributed to Mark Twain, is that the secret to getting ahead is getting started.

To get ahead in life, school, or career, you must be a starter. However, to reach your potential, you must finish some of the things you have started.

Just recently, I was in conversation with a good friend, Annie, who had done some reflecting on her life's journey and how she is now moving ahead because she is learning how to be a better finisher. She was always a good starter but a poor finisher. My friend did not finish high school because of illness and did not feel comfortable returning after her peers had graduated. In time, Annie found work in the energy industry and then resigned after a dozen or so paycheques. She used the money she earned to enrol in an accounting course.

You can guess the outcome. Annie did not last very long.

My friend decided to delve a bit deeper into this negative pattern of behaviour by looking at her family. There, Annie noticed the same pattern. She grew up in a family of great starters who never made it to the finish line. She had no one to look up to as a role model. When you see success, it can motivate or inspire you to keep moving forward. When you don't see it or experience it yourself, it can be defeating and demotivating.

Today, Annie is a certified early childhood educator and just recently graduated as a certified teacher in Ontario. She completed her upgrading course, one assignment at a time. She is a better finisher today than she was yesterday. Why is that?

"Start one thing at a time and finish one thing at a time" became Annie's motto.

How do you be successful if you have no real training, lousy role models, and little time invested? You can't, and this is precisely why so many of our activities fall short of raising the roof.

> **We need to focus in on the present, rather than the future, if we want to finish.**

In fact, modern physics has shown that time's linear sequence of past and future is an illusion. Though at first it may seem abstract to think in this way, the direct practicality of this truth can save you from great suffering. The truth is that time, in its linear sequence of past and future, is something our minds make up. When you see by reference to the past and the future, you will be seeing something that is not there. At first, this may sound like mumbo-jumbo, but go deeper into it and you will begin to understand and be free of something that confines so many of us: time.

Are you a better starter of things than a finisher of things?

Do you know people who are better at finishing what they have started than they are at starting something?

We need to focus in on the present, rather than the future, if we want to finish. Imagine that you have three lenses you can choose to look through. The decision you make about which lens to use determines if you reach the finish line.

• **The first lens focuses on the past.** The past can be clouded with negative memories, resentments, shame, and guilt for what you forgot to do, what you didn't do well, and what went wrong, as well as thoughts about how you should have made changes in your life sooner. When you hold this lens up to your eye, it is difficult to see what's happening now because of all the layers of the past getting in the way. The result is that you can't see what you should do right now. "If only . . . then" beliefs represent a way of thinking about the past. When you engage in "If only . . . then" thinking, you firmly believe that "*If only* _____ had (or hadn't) happened, *then* I could be happy." Here, you are creating a reality for yourself where happiness is impossible because of something in the past that you can no longer control.

• **The second lens looks to the future.** This lens is defective because what will happen in the future is too far away to see clearly. This lens greatly reduces your ability to see clearly what is happening right now because everything you can spot through this lens is tiny and unknown. The result is that you are confused. This is "When . . . then" thinking. Through this lens, you believe that your goal of happiness is conditional upon something happening in the future. Here, you are essentially putting off your happiness until a certain set of conditions are met, and even if those conditions are met, it is highly likely that you will soon come up with yet another "When . . . then," creating a life where you are on an endless hamster wheel and never arriving. It is a curious thing; we demand a certain future so we can be happy, but then, even if we get what we thought we wanted, we make another demand. Thus, every moment is filled with an expectation and we live a life that lacks fulfillment.

• **The third lens puts the spotlight on the present moment.** This lens is clean and clear, allowing you to see yourself and what you have to do right now. That's because the present is right here in front of you, close enough to touch.

Thinking through the lenses of the past and future is called "quicksand thinking." Just as that term suggests, it means stepping into a camouflaged and dangerous pit from which it is near impossible to lift ourselves out when we don't focus on the present moment.

The first step in getting out of quicksand thinking is to recognize that you have fallen into it. This may seem obvious, but when we are engaged in such thinking, we are pretty darn convinced we are right. Even if our faulty thinking is pointed out to us, we are not typically quick to acknowledge it. It is difficult to see you have a bug in your eye when you have a bug in your eye.

To assist with this, begin to identify your "If only . . . then" and "When . . . then" thinking. The following are lists of common "If only . . . then" and "When . . . then" statements that are often heard in the world. Have you caught yourself saying any of these?

"If Only . . . Then" Beliefs

- ▶ *If only* I had done (or not done) what I did, *then* I could be successful and happy.
- ▶ *If only* I was not under so much pressure, *then* I could be more effective and have time to do what makes me happy.
- ▶ *If only* I'd had better support, *then* I would not be so stressed out.
- ▶ *If only* I had a better relationship, *then* I would be happy.
- ▶ *If only* I had a different job, *then* I would feel motivated and happier.
- ▶ *If only* my family life had been different, *then* I would have the life I want.

"When . . . Then" Beliefs

▶ *When* someone else stops doing what they are doing, *then* I will be happier.

▶ *When* someone else starts doing what I want them to do, *then* I will be happier.

▶ *When* I have more money, *then* I will be able to meet my commitments and be happier.

▶ *When* I get promoted, *then* I will be happier.

▶ *When* I am back from vacation, *then* I will be able to relax more.

▶ *When* I find the right position, *then* I will be happy.

▶ *When* I find the right partner, *then* I will be happy.

When you are in quicksand, if you are smart enough to stay still, you might hope that somebody will throw you a vine. But you don't need to rely on someone else to get you out of it. You have the power within you. All you need to do is stop panicking, relax your body, accept the predicament, and spread your arms and legs. Then your body will rise to the top of the quicksand and you can crawl out.

When you find yourself in quicksand thinking, be still and focus on the present moment and what you can do right now.

Remind yourself, "This way of thinking is sinking me!"

Next, consciously choose to change the way you think. Focus on the present and what you are grateful for right now, no matter how small, even if it is just gratitude for the breath you are taking. Sounds so simplistic, but it works! In short, the key to getting out of quicksand thinking is to not panic but be still, recognize your "If only . . . then" and "When . . . then" thinking, and try this new approach.

Doing: Be Present and Listen

Train yourself to be present so that you can get from start to finish.

Listening authentically teaches you to identify the present moment. It is one of the most powerful actions you can initiate in your life.

You may say, "But, Karl, I'm trying to raise my roof! What does listening have to do with dreaming, believing, and doing?"

To that I would say, "Everything!" Here's what happens when we are present and listening:

▶ We have to stop our minds in order to focus.

▶ We wait before we respond.

▶ We are likely to learn new things, because information from outside ourselves is coming in.

▶ We seek to understand things from the point of view of someone else.

▶ Try a little experiment in order to focus on actively listening and build your present-moment skills.

▶ Active listening means that you listen to other people with the full intention of understanding them. It is best to try this with a friend or family member, but you can also try it when you are listening to a radio interview or a podcast.

▶ For this experiment, let go of any criticism you might have of the person doing the talking. Don't try to figure out any solutions to what they are saying. Simply listen. Make eye contact, relax your body, and set an unhurried mood. This way, you communicate to the speaker that you want to know their perspective and experience.

▶ If you give verbal responses, let them be centred on trying to understand the other person, as opposed to arguing or offering your opinion or advice. This experiment can be challenging because really listening requires slowing down.

▶ Practise active listening and other people will feel loved and accepted by you. And you will feel like you were just given wings.

▶ Think of the present moment as the place where the seeds to your success and happiness have been placed. These seeds are kept safe for you to find, even when you are looking elsewhere for them. The past and the future are where the ego leads you on a wild goose chase for your happiness. Vow to look elsewhere.

Exercise Your Potential: Deciding

Once you have become comfortable with the present, you will easily reach the finish line. The following decisions will help you along the way.

Decide: *I will do the best I can in all situations and find ways each day to raise my roof.*

Many people complain that they don't know how to get from start to finish. They cite many common reasons, such as not caring anymore about what comes next, feeling that nothing seems very important, and believing that nobody appreciates their efforts. If this sounds like you, then decide today to stop only thinking about the reasons you can't get things done and begin to do the very best you can, and, most importantly, find ways to put your potential to work.

I know, I know. You may still screw it up. We all do. We all make choices that are imperfect. But if you tell yourself that you are capable of doing your best in all situations, you will have the opportunity to practise raising your roof. You'll also have the ability to make a choice to take a day off from trying so hard. Either way, you'll be putting your potential to work.

This last piece—putting your potential to work—is not something that most people think about with intention. However, as you begin to focus less on the reasons you are unsatisfied and more on reaching your potential and bringing kindness, compassion, and love to at least one interaction each day, the path will unfold before you.

Decide: *Whatever is happening RIGHT NOW, I can learn from it and create opportunity.*

Have you ever noticed how two individuals may be in similar circumstances but do very different things with the experience? For example, two people work hard and expend the same amount of energy and resources to launch a company. They have similar financial results but different reactions to those results. If neither company truly takes off, one person may become bitter and blame others, while the other person uses the experience as a way to learn and create future opportunities. The defining mindset is to not think of yourself as a victim. Instead, learn from what is happening and create further opportunity. Remember, opportunity is most profoundly a result of a growth mindset, not a situation or a condition.

Decide: *I will keep perspective and see the bigger picture of my life. The outcome of my job situation will not make or break my life.*

Many people tie their potential for growth to that of their company or their job. That is, they view the survival of their business or job and their personal survival as one and the same. They cannot imagine being happy if their company does not make it or their job ends, and that leads to constant fear. In short, their identity is mistakenly seen as being tied to what they do. The key perspective that leads to more life satisfaction is to know you can choose to be calm inside and to be kind and compassionate regardless of what happens outside. Although external change, such as a job loss or change in your family life, may be important, the most important thing you can address is the way you think in every single moment. This way, your happiness falls within your control. Typically, the quickest way to reduce stress and experience more success is to stop listening to fear. Realize that even though you may care deeply about your job, you have worth beyond its success or failure.

Decide: *Being patient, kind, truthful, and understanding are essential to raising my roof.*

Becoming sidetracked and stressed by a multitude of tasks and problems and losing sight of what really matters in the long run is easy. In the increasingly complicated work world, it can seem that reacting quickly to endless problems, emptying the inbox as much as possible, and keeping as many balls in the air as you can are the most important tasks. Few retirees, regardless of how successful they were while working, look back on their careers and say, "I wish I had been a little less patient and more of a tyrant." In fact, most look back and see the value of traits such as patience, kindness, honesty, and understanding and wish they had taken more time to develop these. Use the wisdom of their perspective to create the job satisfaction you want now; you will be happier in your job even when things are not going right.

There is no one right-or-wrong set of rules to being happy and successful, no one-size-fits-all ideology or business plan.

There is no guru or leader who will save you from yourself: you (and perhaps a loving force beyond this world) must do this.

Today, there is only you and me and this precious moment, and what we decide to do with it is up to us.

Start one thing at a time and finish one thing at a time. Water your dreams and give them sunshine.

That's how we grow our dream tree.

PART V

THE
MAGIC
YOU

CHAPTER 19

Be the Mirror

A friend of mine called me, and, surprise, surprise! The topic of the call wasn't about getting together for lunch (he owed me one). It was about his recent promotion at work. Lindsay was taking on a management role for the first time.

People reach out to me for a lot of reasons. As a personal growth coach, I often get asked for feedback on how to navigate questions about the challenges we face in life. And that's okay. I feel blessed to be asked for help.

Lindsay was getting ready to speak to an employee, and he was trying to figure out what to say.

"I've been noticing that one of my legacy hires isn't happy at work," he said to me. "He just isn't on the same wavelength as the rest of the team, and he seems isolated. But he does really good work, and so I need to find out what happened."

In a recent meeting, Lindsay had witnessed an interaction between his employee and the rest of the team that didn't sit right with him, and so he thought he would have to say something about it, and soon. He sensed how upset the employee was about the situation, probably because he was singled out by the rest of the team and blamed for something outside of his control.

"It wasn't his fault, though," Lindsay explained. "If there's one thing I can say about our company's performance planning and metrics, it's that they create an emotionally charged environment for everyone. There's so much electricity in the office, it could light up a room for a year. Our approach to performance can make many of us feel overwhelmed, and I know it has to change."

"What's going on?" I asked. "When we're talking about meeting our potential, either as individuals or as a team, we shouldn't need to become overwhelmed with emotion. And we shouldn't be putting the blame on one person's shoulders alone."

"Yeah, I agree. It's like I'm watching this team journeying towards the edge of Niagara Falls with all the tears and angst, especially heading into year-end. I've got to fix this culture of emotion around performance metrics."

"You know what stands out for me?" I asked. "The focus of your actions should be on what's happening right now and what you can do immediately. It's going to take time to create a new performance plan for the team. But if you want to change the culture, that's going to have to start with one person and it's going to have to start right now."

"That makes sense." Lindsay nodded. "I have to help my employee feel supported. I don't want him to leave before I have a chance to change the status quo."

"Ask your employee how you can raise his roof for him. Today."

"What do you mean?"

"Your employee is going to have many good days and many bad days. So are you. Feelings come up and go down like the sun, you know what I mean?"

"Yes," Lindsay said.

"Right now, your employee doesn't know where to turn. Let him turn to you. Hear him out. Offer to listen. Tell him what you value about his work. Ask him what he needs to feel supported, directly. And then follow through. You'll get insight into what's going wrong, fast. It could be the start of a huge change in how you manage your team."

To raise our roof, we have to acknowledge our emotions and

tend to them. We have to honour them by saying "Hello!" to our emotions because we're going to have challenging experiences every day. We can't let other people's criticisms affect who we are and what we decide to do. If someone taps us out of a play, we can take a moment to decide on what we want to do next.

The lesson for Lindsay and his employee was the same. They both had to choose where they wanted to go, not where others wanted to put them.

To take a journey to where they wanted to go, they had to hold a mirror up to themselves, not to other people.

Getting better at anything in life means that you're going to get noticed. When we get noticed, there is a tendency to want to hide. But we can't hide our gifts, and we shouldn't. Reaching our potential gives us the opportunity to inspire others to do the same thing.

When you become who you want to be, you also become a beacon for those around you to meet you where you are.

But to do this, you have to become a mirror for yourself.

When you look in the mirror, you see you—who you are physically to yourself and others.

If you are smiling, we see it.

If you are happy and excited about something, we see it, too.

If you are filled with sadness, we also see that.

> **Getting better at anything in life means that you're going to get noticed.**

What I mean by being a mirror for yourself is to take the time to reflect: seek out reflection from within yourself and seek it out from other people.

A human mirror may see things in you that you don't necessarily see in yourself. After being around a friend for some time, I shared a statement with her that changed her life trajectory. I said with confidence, "I see a teacher in you. You need to release it to do its life's work."

On the other end of the education spectrum, a school board trustee was a mirror for me. He saw the school administrator in me and encouraged me to be a principal.

By showing us what they can accomplish, others may reflect to us what our own potential *might* be. That's inspiring! You may ask yourself, If they can do *that*, then what am I capable of? Most likely, it won't be exactly the same thing. But remember, before that person accomplished what they did for the first time in their own lives, they were also wondering if they would be able to do it.

But a reflecting practice can go even deeper than this.

Neurological research shows that active self-reflection, where people take the time to consciously and continuously reflect on themselves and the needs of those around them, facilitates their ability to relate new information to prior knowledge and seek out new ideas. In empirical research using business case simulations and a reflection-training intervention, a high level of self-reflection correlated with direct performance on the job, as well as increasingly consistent high outcomes in planning and decision-making.[1] Reflecting on what's possible and building a reflective practice, the same findings suggest, allows people to make better decisions even when market conditions are exceptionally challenging. It also directly lowers costs. Reflection helps us decide on what matters most so that we're apt to learn from our experiences.[2]

Why is this?

Research also shows that mindful decision-makers are more open to feedback and less prone to misinterpret it by making self-serving choices, meaning that team engagement and community building can be leveraged to its full potential.[3]

Curiosity can also start with others. A group may become a community when people get to know each other's stories. They also become more aware of the resources that they each present to the team, which opens up doors.

Over time, if practised daily, this approach will lead to personal development that will prepare us for our own future potential. Research shows just how powerful reflection is for future workplace expectations, helping employees internalize broader multi-faceted skills, including creativity, imagination, and entrepreneurship.[4]

The breadth of these research findings is so incredible. We know unequivocally that reflection is a skill that we all need right now.

I have many mirrors around me because I know I need reflection to reach my own potential.

I prefer mirrors to walls. A wall is limiting. When there is a wall around you, day in and day out, you become tired and emotionally drained, leaving you at risk for not achieving your potential. A wall just gets in your way.

But a reflection, now that is helpful.

Are you a mirror or a wall?

See your own reflection.

Are you a person people go to when they're facing a challenge? If the answer isn't yes, then know that building your community, whether at work, in your family, or with your friend group, starts with the mirror.

Are you a person you would want to work for? Reflect on the hard truth of who you are and who you want to be.

To reflect in a way that helps you, you need to see more of the whole picture by learning to observe your own mind.

Think about a time when you were at the movies. You may have become very involved in the film, even to the point of having physical and emotional reactions, such as a pounding heart or shedding tears. Yet, all the while, a part of your mind was clear that you were at the movies, watching a drama unfold in front of you. You never lost the ability to turn your head away or leave altogether.

Now remember, there are movies going on all the time in the theatre of your mind. The film is your thoughts. In this theatre, you often behave as if the movie is real and that there is nothing you can do about your experience. You sit and experience upsetting, shocking, and frightening movies, and don't realize that you are the writer, director, and projectionist.

In those moments, do you recognize that you have the ability to change the film?

I remember discovering and celebrating my ideas and my new-found awareness, but also fighting them at the same time.

Like everyone, my reflections showed me that I had my own legacy patterns. In some cases, I was forced to deal with those points of discomfort. When I am *totally* honest with myself, I recognize that it *really felt good* to tell myself the same stories: why I hadn't achieved a goal that was important to me, why I disagreed with a family member, or why I didn't have time to exercise. The more I told myself the stories, the more I believed them, and the pattern continued. Leaning into my trauma was overpowering my desire to be free of it.

I just had to own it.

Making Magic: Freedom Thoughts

To do this yourself, you need to learn how to be aware of your thoughts without allowing them to run wild. Developing the ability to identify and reflect on your thoughts gives you tremendous freedom and increases your capacity to raise your roof.

The idea is that there is a part of your mind that can watch your thoughts coming and going. You may be able to watch your thoughts as you would watch waves at the beach, coming in, going out. There might be some calm times without many waves, and you just watch the calm. There might be other times with large, crashing waves, and you just watch the dramatic display. Don't reach into the water and grab any of your thoughts. Instead, name them as they float by. Try to have a mental stance that is as detached as possible. Simply watch your thoughts and state what they are about. Suppose, for example, that you are thinking about a money problem. Say to yourself, "Thinking about money," and then move on to whatever else comes into your mind. Try to resist the temptation of delving into any one thought. If you do, simply catch yourself, name the thought, and move on to the next.

When watching your thoughts, remember the following:

▶ You are at the movies. Don't act like all of your personal horror films and action thrillers are real. Remember, your potential growth is real. Play those movies instead.

▶ Know that you can change films any time. You can even rewrite the scripts. Themes of fear and revenge can be switched to themes of love and forgiveness at any time you choose.

▶ Begin to spend time looking at the movie listings prior to going to the movies. Choose your thoughts. The best times to do this are before you go to sleep and before you get out of bed.

Don't be discouraged if this technique takes some time to develop. Learning to reflect and become your own mirror is something that takes patience and perseverance. The payoff is you get to choose the movies.

Taking time for reflection means that we are taking total responsibility for our potential growth.

When we are unafraid to be a mirror to ourselves, we are living with integrity. There is nothing we are hiding from; we are fully ourselves.

Living in integrity can feel like a lot of work on the surface.

In fact, it is a lot of work.

But on the other hand, once you remember how to live life in that way, it becomes easier. And then amazingly simple.

To do this, we have to get rid of the "yeah, . . . but" response in our minds.

Here's how.

Resist searching for ways your potential personal, work, or family success can be taken away. Every time you have a limiting thought—like "Well, yeah, maybe I could be happier, but if I don't get a better job I can't afford anything"—you are giving power to external situations, which prevent you from experiencing happiness and making something positive happen right now.

To get rid of your "yeah, . . . but" thoughts, deal with them the same way as you would control weeds in your yard: by pulling one at a time.

Self-made blocks to reaching our potential—just like weeds— will rapidly grow out of control unless you stop them. Nothing is more important in any given moment than focusing on what you can do and the thoughts you can have to create happiness, rather than on what you can't do and the things you believe will prevent your happiness.

When you have a "yeah, . . . but" moment, ask yourself, "Does this 'yeah, . . . but' have to limit my success and happiness?" You'll quickly realize that it doesn't. You can then reframe your statement to focus on removing the block to happiness. Above all else, teach yourself the power to remove your "yeah, . . . but" by acknowledging that while difficult circumstances may be unavoidable, suffering is optional.

When I have a "yeah, . . . but" moment, what I find helpful is to imagine that I can only think in one of two ways: I can either think of reasons why I cannot be peaceful and happy, or I can think of how, in this present moment right now, I can act towards reaching my potential. All my perceptions, thoughts, and actions will emanate from one thought or the other. The choice I make will determine my experience.

To raise our roof, we have to take total responsibility for our actions. When we can get rid of our excuses, we will be able to live in total integrity. And living highest-integrity versions of ourselves is the way to blow off the top of that roof over our heads.

The mirror is where you can't really lie to yourself and you can't pretend you are someone you are not. You feel it become a part of your life on a cellular level.

You know when you're not living that life of integrity.

Sometimes we might feel that when we live in high integrity, it's foolish because someone could take advantage of our goodness. You know, that's simply a way of justifying our behaviours so that we feel less bad about not meeting ourselves in that place of true self-awareness.

But if you are aspiring towards a high-integrity relationship with yourself, you have to walk in high compassion with yourself at the same time. When you reach the tipping point where you can be no other version of yourself, it becomes easier. Once you're locked in the gravitational field of integrity, you're not getting away.

Taking the time to learn to observe your mind through reflection and see your thoughts for what they are is critical to reaching your potential.

With practice, in any moment, you can take notice of the stream of thoughts, images, and ideas moving into your awareness and do so without attaching yourself to them, without arguing for or against them. This is the beginning of experiencing your mind in a conscious manner, rather than being unconsciously ruled by it; it is the start of choice, of becoming aware of your mind, which is a prerequisite for any lasting happiness and harmony.

Don't underestimate how much your mind can keep you stuck when you remain an unconscious participant in your own thoughts!

Only through bringing an increasing awareness to the mind can you have any hope of transcending your unquestioned fear and becoming free of all of your personal blocks to raising your roof.

Exercise Your Potential: Your Imagination Portfolio

Become the director of your own mind.

Create a reflection portfolio. This is a physical object. It could be like a journal but filled with answers to specific questions, like:

How do you want people to see you?

What is your greatest virtue?

What is your personal code of ethics?

It could also be something more visual, with pictures, clippings, and anything related to your friction points.

Imagine all of the big things that inspire you, and make space for them in your portfolio.

CHAPTER 20

Shimmer like Gold

During their childhood, I saw my children as if they were tiny, heavy drops of gold.

On almost any given day, after walking into my home after work, I would see them working and playing with such intensity. It was as if they were gold nuggets in a stream, fallen and hidden deep amongst the water and rocks. That is how immersed they were in their tasks.

Every day after school, each of my five children were doing their thing.

My eldest daughter would have a copy of her Goosebumps book in her hands, a book series that swallowed her up.

My second daughter would have a paintbrush. Little cups of paint along with an easel holding a piece of canvas furnished her world, the playground for her imagination and creativity.

One of my sons would be sitting on the couch taping his stick. There was nothing routine about his work. The stick was an extension of his being. The roll of tape was more than a roll of tape. He was getting the stick ready to do magic on the ice.

Another son was dressed in his goalie equipment, on his knees making imaginary saves. He made it professionally because he learned to make saves in his mind, then on the ice.

My youngest son spent his childhood working to catch up to his big brothers and sisters. He would have a whistle in his mouth while he stickhandled socks made into a ball and deke to score into the empty laundry basket. When we were tired of the whistle blowing, we hid the whistle. He was so determined that he would find the whistle to continue playing in his world.

Just like the sun and moon rising, and setting and fading away, in the sky above, I hardly noticed that my children were doing their work. I never thought much of it, but doing their thing worked to shape my children. Everything they immersed themselves in became something they were good at doing. Everything they did made them shimmer like gold. They needed my love. But their love for themselves had to shine from within before their outward lives could shine.

When you discover what you love doing and become skilled at doing it, you tend to do more, be more, and become more in your life. As they got older, my children's tasks became heavier, but still, they remained immersed. I remember having a lot of conversations about what we could do to lessen the burden but still ensure they had fun.

At the same time, I also knew when I had to let go. If my children were going to continue to shine, they had to do things on their own.

"I can teach you, but I can't learn or skate for you."

"I can show you something, but I can't see it for you."

"I can tell you something, but I can't hear it for you."

"I can't do your dream for you or go where you want to go for you."

"I will not make excuses for you, but I will pave the way for you to go the distance."

"I can't go to school for you or to the gym or track to do your laps for you."

"I can see the potential in you. I hope you can see it, too."

My three hockey sons went far up the hockey ladder. They had to step up their ability to look, listen, and pay attention, focusing on becoming gold. This story is about PK, but it could easily have been about Malcolm or Jordan. During one of PK's skating sessions with his team, the skating coach called him over and instructed him to take a knee, a common routine when meeting on the ice during the teaching and learning sessions. After PK took his pose and was ready, the coach asked him if he wanted to go far in hockey, school, and life. There were no doubts in his mind.

His answer was a resounding yes!

"Well, PK, if you want to go far, you better learn how to listen and pay attention to what you are being taught or instructed to do."

I shared the same wisdom with my students at school.

"Do you want to go far in life?" I would ask them. All hands went up quickly and voluntarily. No one looked around to see which hands were up. This question works the same way when adults are in the room. Every one of us wants to achieve our goals.

"If that's the case, then you have to focus," I always say in return to their raised hands.

When my boys were younger, they played house league in Etobicoke, Ontario. I can still hear the voice of one hockey parent chanting out, "Focus! Focus! Focus!" Each time her son stepped on the ice for his three-minute shift, she began her chant and ended when her young son stepped off the ice.

We can't shine unless we do our thing. To get to the gold in life, you need to shine brightly.

Every one of us can shine like the sun and moon.

To reach your potential, you must find your own world and live in it. This is the world that inspires you to learn, grow, and develop more. You must work to make what you imagine real so that you can go beyond the clouds and become a shining beacon of light for others.

Children are good at making their imaginations come to life, and I think we have a lot to learn from them. They do not see the limitations that we see in ourselves as adults; they simply invent a new way to achieve their goals.

The reason it's important to remember your playtime skills right now, as you near the end of this book, is that this is a lesson I don't want you to forget.

Play is something that we adults do forget much of time, but for educators like me, it is the golden ticket. Research shows the following truths for both children and adults:

- There is a definitive link between play and the development of skills connected with creativity and emotional intelligence.
- Play helps people develop more effective social skills as well as confidence in their own abilities.
- Play assists everyone with whole-language development, which is the use of integrated listening, speaking, reading, and writing.

Play can lead to innovation and positive change for society as a whole.

To get to that gold, think like a child: create the kind of confidence and happiness that is aligned with being immersed in doing *your* thing. With practice, like a child at play, you can take notice of the stream of thoughts, images, and ideas moving into your awareness at any moment and use them to advance your own ideas and grow towards your dream future.

To get to the gold in life, you need to shine brightly.

Making Magic: Play Wonderful Games

Think about the kinds of statements that a child might say to themselves if they were able to articulate their playtime focus:

▶ There is nothing I lack to feel confidence and peace of mind right now.

▶ I am focused inside, regardless of what's happening in the space around me.

▶ Whatever is happening, I can learn from it.

▶ The most important thing I am doing is what I can see in front of me right now. The past is over and the future is not yet here.

▶ Patience and understanding lead to fun and success, all at the same time.

▶ Sharing with others increases happiness, confidence, and results.

A child's play practice is innovative, exciting, and healing in that it provides a real chance to make a new beginning. This core practice to raising your roof is about your ability to shimmer like gold.

As adults, however, we find it all too easy to become sidetracked and lose sight of what really matters: our basis for happiness. In this increasingly complicated world, you need to remind yourself of your potential to grow, and the more you develop this awareness, the more confident and happier you will be.

What if, like a young child at play, you had no problems, only opportunities? How would your life be different then? For children, everything is wide open and possible. There is never a circumstance, no matter how challenging or time-consuming, that also does not hold within it an opportunity to make things better, to better yourself. Every moment is an opportunity to love, to learn, and to grow beyond your dreams.

Let's take a moment to measure whether or not you're currently able to connect with the growth skills you learned as a child.

Exercise Your Potential: Childhood Gold

Can you tap into childhood gold? Here's a quiz to get you on your way.

1. How often do you start your day cultivating a positive mindset and setting a positive intention that makes you excited to get started on your day?

    0 = never
    1 = almost never
    2 = sometimes
    3 = fairly often
    4 = very often

2. How often during the day do you take breaks from work to imagine, create, or explore by taking part in a non-media-related hobby or activity?

    0 = never
    1 = almost never
    2 = sometimes
    3 = fairly often (every three to four hours)
    4 = very often (every two hours)

3. How often during the week do you take at least a thirty-minute walk in nature, in a park, or around the block, or how often do you play a game outdoors, such as street hockey, basketball or Frisbee?

0 = never
1 = almost never
2 = sometimes (once a week)
3 = fairly often (three times a week)
4 = very often (five times a week)

4. How often are you able to spend time with people doing an activity you all enjoy?

0 = never
1 = almost never
2 = sometimes (once a week)
3 = fairly often (three times a week)
4 = very often (five times a week)

5. How often are you able to change direction when you are doing something that you do not enjoy?

0 = never
1 = almost never
2 = sometimes (once a week)
3 = fairly often (three times a week)
4 = very often (five times a week)

6. How high do you rank contentment with your activities as a goal on a daily basis?

0 = zero priority
1 = a low priority
2 = an aspirational priority that I have difficulty attaining
3 = a fairly high priority that I long for more of
4 = a very high priority that I work towards every day

7. How high do you rank personal happiness as a goal on a daily basis?

0 = zero priority
1 = a low priority
2 = an aspirational priority that I have difficulty attaining
3 = a fairly high priority that I long for more of
4 = a very high priority that I work towards every day

Now, make a list of your response numbers and add them up.

If your score is under 14, your lifestyle does not support your ability to connect with your childhood sense of play. Some of your innate potential and happiness is likely to be unrealized. Through a few simple changes, you can achieve more in life, at every level. These can be found later in this chapter.

If your score is between 14 and 20 your lifestyle supports some understanding of the value of play, although not as optimally as it could.

If your score is over 21, your lifestyle supports play at its absolute best, and your heart is likely full and happy.

As you can tell by these questions, I'm not asking you to get down on the floor and play with toy trains (unless you really want to). Instead, I want you to think seriously about the kind of intentions you set to bring positive non-work activities into your life and how you commit to them.

We're not machines, but sometimes we feel like them!

We need to build in time for daily activities where we get to explore our immersion in something that is just for us. Play makes us human, and it makes us better as humans.

You've probably never heard of Kutol Products, but back in the 1930s, they were big deal in household cleaning in the United States. They had revolutionized wall and wallpaper cleaners, a necessity in houses heated by coal and wood fires. Their putty-like non-toxic cleaners removed sooty buildup on all surfaces, quickly and easily. Like the Dyson vacuum cleaners of the present day, Kutol experimented a lot to get their products right and were always on the cutting edge. But twenty years later, after the end of World War II and the development of new forms of electric home heating, Kutol's product sales sagged.

Taking over the business in the 1950s, Joseph McVicker needed to find a way to make Kutol work again, and he had almost given up when his sister-in-law Kay Zufall, a teacher, brought a ball of wallpaper cleaner into her Cincinnati kindergarten classroom and handed it over to the children.[1]

Within minutes, the kids were making the putty into fanciful shapes: they were moulding it into castles, dogs, and clowns.

The kids wanted to know what the putty was called. The name, Zufall said, was Play-Doh.

Within months, McVicker was rolling out a new line of children's toys, colouring the putty and selling it in its now-familiar tubs. It was so popular that it reached stores across the whole nation a few years later, and today more than three billion cans of the product have been sold. Play-Doh, now owned by Hasbro, has even been honoured in the National Toy Hall of Fame.

What can we learn from this story?

What Zufall taught us, and what I also know from my own work in teaching, is that kids don't see the limitations by which we, as adults, feel constricted. McVicker would likely never have considered moving his company towards toy production if Zufall hadn't made a choice to hand his wallpaper putty over to her students. Being open to play means we can move in any direction, like a queen on a chessboard. Kids are not bound by the rules of any game at all. If we are interested in reaching our potential, we ought to be aiming to become personally agile through play.

It's just like when Eric Schmidt was CEO at Google. In that role, he instituted the 70:20:10 ratio for innovation. It works pretty simply.

► 70 percent of employees' time should be dedicated to core business tasks.
► 20 percent should be dedicated to projects related to the core business.
► 10 percent should be dedicated to projects unrelated to the core business.

What this means is that least 10 percent of the work being done at Google is wholly unconnected to employees' job titles or responsibilities. The company specifically built in space to allow for this freedom. The results of this experience taught Google that nobody wants to pretend when they come to the office. No one wants to leave parts of their personality at home. People want to express themselves, be fully present in the workplace, and feel free to explore ideas that are unique to their own interests.

Here are four ways in which you can start using your childlike skills to shimmer like gold.

• **Use the "clear" button.** As human beings, we are capable of elevating all sorts of stressful events purely in our heads, exciting our negative emotions and producing everyday fear. Most of these reactions are tied to mere thoughts, often not based on reality. But there are easy ways for us to quiet our thinking.

Imagine that you have a "clear" button, a tool that can stop stressful thinking right away. When fearful or anxious thoughts arise, visualize this button at the centre of your palm and press it. It will send a signal to calm the primitive part of the brain that generates anxiety and stress. Keep pressing the button. Psychologists call this process "anchoring." After practising it several times, even though the button is pretend, it begins to have a real physical effect.

Then, count to three. The part of your brain that launches stress reactions has the intelligence of a two-year-old, and like a two-year-old, it needs to be distracted. Counting to three will do the trick. You can also imagine each number as a colour. See one as red, two as yellow and three as green, taking a slow, easy breath with each number you count.

On the final breath, let go. Feel yourself relax. Bring your attention to the present moment and consciously adopt a gentle, almost unperceivable smile from the inside.

• **Make space for quiet.** Start the day in quiet. Feel appreciation for the gift of another day of life. Set your intention to have a great day, filled with happiness and sustained through an attitude that is grateful and loving.

During the day, take nature breaks (every two hours is ideal). Step outside or just look out the window for a minute or two and let your problems go completely. Watch something in nature, such as the clouds shifting or the wind blowing. Connect with life and have compassion for yourself for a moment. Once a week, before going to sleep, count your blessings. Name three things that happened in the previous week for which you are grateful.

• **Take your brain for a walk.** Walking or doing a fun physical activity outside for thirty minutes a day flushes stress hormones from your body and oxygenates your brain. (Aim for five days a week, but if that feels daunting, then start off with once or twice a week.) People who walk regularly show significant improvement in memory skills and even tend to be happier. When you are walking, try these things:

▶ Imagine each inhale softening and opening your heart and each exhale expanding your awareness of the world around you.
▶ Notice simple things, like colours, sounds, and smells, and feel sensations such as the wind touching your cheeks.
▶ Observe one new thing about the neighbourhood on every walk and write it down in a journal when you get home.

• **Break your routine.** Doing something new or different helps the brain stay young and the heart become happier. Break the mould of old routines. Mostly, stop thinking in ways that say you don't have enough or can't reach your potential. When you are feeling blocked, give to others through service, even if only in some small way. Remember, potential is magic because with it, you can reach more, do more, and become more. Potential is the beauty that we each possess inside of us.

Your dreams are gold. When you raise that roof, when you look outside and the clouds clear, you can see a rainbow of possibilities.

CHAPTER 21

Up and Beyond

The day was so dark, it was as if it were night.

There was no one, nothing, in sight.

Nothing at all. No birds singing, chirping, or flying nearby.

No sun in the sky.

The Old Man could hear the voice of nature, the whistling wind striking fear in him, disrupting and distracting his thoughts. He worried for a moment that the wind would break through, shaping and shifting the clothes on his back.

He was holding on. He was determined not to be blown away or subtracted from existence.

But then, the Old Man looked at the giant tree, tall above him, shaking like a dancer out of control on a dance floor.

"Grow," he said to the tree. "Your branches are looking naked, weak, and tired. Leaves have been blown off and are now slaves to the wind."

The Old Man thought for a second that the wind seemed to be in control of Grow, in a fight for its stability. He could see through the top of the roof, and just like a boxer, Grow was taking some hard blows. Punches were coming at the tree from everywhere. They were hitting their targets and leaving a mark.

But the Old Man was not worried.

He knew that everything was just fine.

He looked up and talked to Grow again.

"There is something that belongs to the trees and something in each of us that is keeping us standing. We bend but do not break; we bend but do not get knocked down," the old man said, patting Grow on its sturdy trunk.

"Your root system keeps you from being uprooted from your place, and, even more, from *yourself*. You are anchored when you find yourself in a season of storm."

The Old Man looked to the roof, and he felt secure. Even though Grow's tendrils and branches had made their way past the roof and into the blustering sky, he himself felt sheltered. He knew he was safe. He had tended Grow so carefully and calmly that the tree had reached its ultimate potential.

It had branches to spare, branches that fluttered, secure against any blows.

It had leaves so thick, they clustered as a shield against the wind.

It had roots so deep that the house around it did not shudder at all.

Grow was well anchored, and so are we.

"When the root is deep, there is no reason to fear the wind," an old African proverb tells us.

There will be seasons of storms. Going through difficult times is normal. Sometimes, you, me, and everyone else will be in one of life's storms. There are days that will be darker, leaving us feeling lost, weak, and tired.

But, in supporting our dream tree, there is nothing that we cannot do, in sunshine and in rain.

If we have done the work to raise our roof, then the dream trees that we have nurtured will always protect us from storms.

Our dream tree will bear flowers and fruit, nectar and nourishment.

Our dream tree will give us shade when we need it.

Our dream tree will provide us with a ladder to the sun, the moon, and the stars.

And all storms that rock its branches will be temporary. They will pass.

In growing to reach our potential, we too have created a root system that runs deep in the soul of our being. Our roots will always keep us anchored when we believe in ourselves. The greater the belief, the deeper our roots run and the stronger our branches become in the stormy seasons of life. When we feel shaken off the path to reaching our maximum potential, we must trust in our potential just as the Old Man trusted in Grow. We should never lose our grip, because we will never be lost even when we find ourselves blowing around in the wind of change. You were made to be a dreamer, a believer, and a doer.

Remember, when we change, we grow. And when we grow, we change.

Think about the core questions I asked you to consider at the beginning of this journey.

1. When it comes to your personal growth and development, how much time and effort are you willing to give?
2. What is one thing that you can change today to feel a little bit better about yourself?
3. If you were the old man in the story, what decision would you have made to clear the way for the plant to grow to its full potential?
4. Are you comfortable under your roof? Are you a roof-buster?
5. What steps are you taking to learn, grow, and develop past your roof?

Have your answers to those questions changed from when you first started reading this book? How has your perspective changed on what is possible for you? Can you see your dream tree in your mind? What is the first thing you are going to do when you set this book down?

Before you set it down, it's time once again for you to say those six magic words: "I believe in my own potential."

Say those words loud and proud. "I believe in my own potential."

Say them again! "I believe in my own potential."

You were made to be a dreamer, a believer, and a doer.

I believe in your potential. The world believes in your potential. The seeds of growth are at your fingertips. Now, after reading this book, I hope very much that you believe in your own potential and that you remember who you are: you are the dream you create.

How are you going to raise your roof today?

DREAM IT!

BELIEVE IT!

WORK IT!

LIVE IT!

CELEBRATE IT!

DO IT OVER AGAIN!

ACKNOWLEDGEMENTS

This book would not have been possible without the help and support of my team of all-stars.

Thank you to everyone involved in its development and production. Elle Glencoe, you inspired me more than you can ever imagine. We were always on the same page, moving in the right direction, thanks to your leadership, skills, and vision. Carolyn Forde, my agent, you see the person and the vision in my books. Your leadership, guidance, and unwavering support were instrumental. Brad Wilson, my editor and my coach, your feedback, intelligence, and critical examination of the words in this book from cover to cover were invaluable to this team. I also want to say thank you to the rest of the HarperCollins Canada team who worked tirelessly behind the scenes. Your ideas, creativity, and talents have made a difference in my life.

Thank you, as well, to my coaching clients, my students, and the organizations to whom I dedicate my time. You are my guiding stars and the reasons I get up every day aiming to raise my own roof. I want to give a special thanks to Cal Belbin, who shared some wonderful personal growth experiences with me and asked a lot of great questions.

Finally, I want to thank my family, who continue to inspire me to reach my maximum potential. Without you, I would never have learned the skills of teaching, mentoring, and coaching. The incredible stories I am able to share about your achievements continue to inspire others.

APPENDIX: RAISE THEIR ROOF

Playbooks for Leaders, Parents, and Teachers

Lauren Rowles is a British parasport rower and former wheelchair athlete. She won gold at the 2016 Summer Paralympics in Rio and again at the games in Tokyo in 2021. At thirteen years old, Rowles was diagnosed with a rare neurological condition and suddenly paralyzed from the waist down. She's also a part of the LGBTQ+ community. Her childhood dream was to be an Olympic athlete, but navigating her perceived differences made her path to gold very unique. She saw Paralympians on television, but the coverage left her feeling bleak about her prospects.

"Sports is a strange place, because it reflects our roles in life," Rowles said. "In some places, it's not the most inclusive, and in others, it feels like the only place you belong."

That's why Rowles is leveraging her own story to get more people with disabilities and more LGBTQ+ youth involved in sports.

"That's my vision now," Rowles told her sponsors at Adidas. "It's not a physical, tangible thing. I'm focused on winning, but I'm also focused on this wider thing of what gives me purpose, what fulfills me. In the end you hope that you can inspire someone to go down this sporting path and that they go on to do much greater things than you ever did."[1]

Rowles's story inspired me so much. Her work isn't just about getting to gold, that potential win most athletes crave. Instead, what gives her purpose is raising the roof for others and making more room for people to enjoy the freedom of competing in a sport they love.

Raising your roof and raising the roof for everyone else can be one and the same thing. Making that roof so high that everyone can be invited over, so that you can have a house party, should be a goal for all of us.

I'm going to outline some ways in which you can start doing just that.

These handy playbooks have been specifically designed for organizational leaders, for parents, and for teachers. They contain tips and tools for raising the roof for people you influence: employees, kids, and students. You may also be able to use these guides to help others in any relationships in your life.

Raise Their Roof: A Playbook for Leaders

To raise their roof, put employees first.

If a leader's intention is to advance the agenda of the organization without really listening to employees, they will create an echo chamber. Is that going to work? Does controlling employees lead to a better bottom line? It doesn't. However, if we're in a leadership position, we often automatically assume that we know what's best for others.

Instead, a leader's intention should be to validate and connect with each employee, allowing for authentic interactions that lead to creative thinking among all team members. Employees should go home at the end of each day excited to be there the next.

Ask yourself the following questions, and be honest with yourself about the answers.

▶ When I am in conversation, how much of the time am I listening and asking questions and how much do I speak?

▶ When I set goals, what are the ways in which I achieve them? Am I open to various ways to achieve these goals or am I focused only on the ways I already know?

▶ When I listen to employees, can I maturely deal with negative feelings along with positive ones? Can I reflect authentically on the lessons others are trying to teach me?

▶ When I lead a meeting, do I listen to the various voices of my employees or mainly speak about my own agenda?

▶ Do I dare to put others' ideas into action, giving them credit for the hard work and professional risk they have put into sharing their best efforts?

▶ When I am not sure what to do next, have I asked my employees to contribute?

Now that you've reflected on your own role, think about how to put this new perspective into action. Bring to mind a pattern of working behaviour, thought, or action that has served its purpose and is now limiting your ability to raise the roof for others. Reflect on that habit and ways you can change it.

Try out the following ideas to support growth in your organization:

▶ Be open to asking for feedback from your employees regarding what works and what doesn't work, and implement their suggested changes.

▶ Create a workplace environment that nourishes continuous learning. Offer your employees the training and development programs *of their choice* to acquire new skills and sharpen their approach to work, based on *their own* professional goals.

▶ Use stand-up meetings, a ten-minute gathering in which everyone shares what he or she is working on right now, and see where you can provide support for each employee.

▶ Make a routine in which every month or so, depending on your schedule, you meet with a new employee to ask about their goals and how they need support. Stay curious and open-minded about each individual and their wishes.

▶ Acknowledge the process and the investment people are putting into their work. Even if it's a challenging time, amplify the good. Try to see and show your team the opportunities that connect their work to the success of the organization and also to their own professional development.

▶ Award individuals for meeting their own goals and raising their roof, not just that of the company. Engagement is much more likely when people are doing things that matter to them personally, not just filling in time at a job to make ends meet.

Raise Their Roof: A Playbook for Parents

As a parent, you may think that you need to help your child raise their roof, and, in many ways, you must. At the same time, you can't water their dream tree for them. You can't open their windows. If you do, you're only going to feed your own sapling, not theirs. That's the most important thing about your child reaching their own potential: making space for their own journey to unfold.

Think about raising the roof for your child as a stream that flows between two banks of a river. The water touches each side, and yet on each, there are different rocks, plants, and flowers. That flow of water can reach a larger pool if you work together to each shape part of the riverbed, but it will become constricted if you work at cross purposes to your child.

So, how can you actually help your child? What will make that river of creativity and opportunity flow more fully?

▶ Be present mentally, emotionally, and physically. Bring yourself to this relationship fully, every single day. Even if you're tired and frustrated with other things in life, know that your child depends on your ability to see them through the lens of love.

▶ Share how you see things and share what you feel and experience about your child through dialogue, rather than by telling them what to do.

▶ Dare to be vulnerable. Have the courage to bring your authentic viewpoint and feelings into your relationship with your child at an age-appropriate level, in order to build their trust in you.

▶ Open your mind and heart to new ideas and views, put your assumptions aside, and listen with curiosity to their ideas. Be open to letting go of your assumptions and enabling new wisdom to emerge.

▶ Respect your child. Make space for their ideas and opinions, even if at first you feel the urge to contradict them. Pause and listen, especially when your overwhelming feelings are those of inconvenience, exhaustion, or frustration.

▶ If you aren't satisfied with the relationship you have with your child, reflect upon it. Ask yourself how you can change it, not what your child can do to change. What can you do differently that will change the kinds of interactions you have with your child? It doesn't need to be something big: you can change your tone of voice, the time of day you choose to have conversations, or how you offer new ideas.

▶ Bring to mind a pattern of behaviour, thought, or action that has served its purpose and is now limiting how you communicate with your child. Reflect about the habit, ways you can cope, and how to change it.

▶ Manage your own psychological safety and triggers. If conversations with your child trigger you, pause and try to practise compassion for yourself and for them. Try to understand your child's life goals and the pain they themselves are holding when you think they should be doing something different. How can you help?

▶ Maintain uncertainty without setting it aside. Create space for uncertainty within yourself and through dialogue with your child. Don't push for a solution when you are trying to figure out how to help your child reach their potential. It's okay not to know the answers. It's okay not to find a solution right away.

▶ Every morning, be thankful for three things you love about your child. It can be anything you appreciate: their smile, their last school project, the way that they love purple. Don't take anything about your relationship with your child for granted.

Raise Their Roof: Playbook for Teachers

Empathy is at the heart of teaching and at the heart of raising the roof for your students.

A child's ability to acquire compassion and creativity, and raise their own roof is linked not only to their social environment, but also to their personal self-esteem. As a teacher, you need an ability to sense where your students are at in their learning journey and in their life journey at the same time. You need to not only accurately recognize their needs and their wants, you need to care deeply about who your students are as people.

What does this look like in the classroom?

▶ Use direct communication, with a focus on building connection and compassion for how the child is feeling. Each child needs to be seen and heard so that, like little Madison, whom we met earlier on, they can slowly open up and share their ideas with you.

▶ Create opportunities for non-rational learning experiences based on emotions and emotional connection, which involves mutual praise for students' life goals, even if they seem silly. No idea is a bad idea when you are a student of five, or ten, or even fifteen years!

▶ Embrace appreciative inquiry in learning from success instead from failures. Give praise to students for the capabilities and benefits they bring to the table.

▶ Allow your students to spend time to get to know each other, and place a focus on understanding each other. Allow your students to define formal boundaries between them and others through listening and empathy.

▶ Encourage self-management, especially in aspirational learning activities.

Try this exercise. You can easily adapt it for students of all ages.

If you knew that your time was limited, what would you do with the time you have today, this month, and this year? Instead of repeating something you already do, think about something you have never done before. Think about who you would want to spend time with. Why are you thinking about that person or people? What do they add to your life?

Write down (or draw, if children are younger) your definition of a successful and rewarding future. What does your perfect working day look like? What does your perfect weekend look like? Are they similar or different?

And lastly, help your students raise their roof by raising your own.

Find the time to nourish yourself, both inside and outside of the classroom. This can involve practising meditation for five minutes at your desk, taking a break in nature with or without your students, or leading an activity that refuels you, rather than only your students.

Practise listening to yourself. Be attentive and connect to the different emotions that reside in you in every moment. Let them be; enable them space without trying to change them. Just acknowledge them.

NOTES

Introduction

1. Malcolm Gladwell, *Outliers: The Story of Success* (Little, Brown, 2008).
2. Anders Ericsson and Robert Pool, *Peak: Secrets from the New Science of Expertise* (Houghton Mifflin Harcourt, 2016).

Chapter 1: The Man Without a Roof

1. Rebecca L. Collins, "For Better or Worse: The Impact of Upward Social Comparison on Self-Evaluations," *Psychological Bulletin* 119.1 (1996): 51–69, https://psycnet.apa.org/doi/10.1037/0033-2909.119.1.51.

Chapter 2: Look Up

1. Matthew J. Easterbrook and Ian R. Hadden, "Tackling Educational Inequalities with Social Psychology: Identities, Contexts, and Interventions," *Social Issues and Policy Review* 15.1 (2020): 180–236, https://doi.org/10.1111/sipr.12070.
2. Andreas Maercker et al., "Complex Post-Traumatic Stress Disorder," *The Lancet* 400.10345 (July 2022): 60–72, https://doi.org/10.1016/s0140-6736(22)00821-2.
3. U.S. Centers for Disease Control and Prevention, "About Adverse Childhood Experiences," April 9, 2024, https://www.cdc.gov/aces/about/index.html.
4. Elizabeth Swedo et al., "Prevalence of Adverse Childhood Experiences Among U.S. Adults — Behavioral Risk Factor Surveillance System, 2011–2020," *Morbidity and Mortality Weekly Report* 72.26 (June 30, 2023): 707–715, http://dx.doi.org/10.15585/mmwr.mm7226a2.
5. Mark Bellis et al., "Life Course Health Consequences and Associated Annual Costs of Adverse Childhood Experiences Across Europe and North America: A Systematic Review and Meta-Analysis," *Lancet Public Health* 4.10 (September 3, 2019): e517–e528, https://doi.org/10.1016/S2468-2667(19)30145-8.
6. Carol Dweck, "Carol Dweck Revisits the 'Growth Mindset,'" *Education Week* 35.5 (2015): 20–24.

7. Simon Sinek, *Start with Why: How Great Leaders Inspire Everyone to Take Action* (Portfolio, 2009).

Chapter 3: Light Your Flame

1. Martin Luther King Jr., "Keep Moving from This Mountain," April 10, 1960, Spelman College, https://kinginstitute.stanford.edu/king-papers /documents/keep-moving-mountain-address-spelman-college-10-april -1960.

Chapter 4: What Is a Dream?

1. Charles P. Fisher, "Culture and Dreaming: A Story of Co-Creation," *International Journal of Applied Psychoanalytic Studies* 19.2 (2022): 230–240, https://doi.org/10.1002/aps.1742.

2. Sevasti Kapsi, Spyridoula Katsantoni, and Athanasios Drigas, "The Role of Sleep and Impact on Brain and Learning," *International Journal of Recent Contributions from Engineering, Science & IT* 8.3 (2020): 59–68, https://doi.org/10.3991/ijes.v8i3.17099.

3. Martin Oscarsson et al., "A Large-Scale Experiment on New Year's Resolutions: Approach-Oriented Goals Are More Successful than Avoidance-Oriented Goals," *PLoS One* 15.12 (2020): e0234097, https://doi.org/10.1371/journal.pone.0234097.

4. Gretchen Rubin, "Little: Working Is One of the Most Dangerous Forms of Procrastination," *Happier with Gretchen Rubin*, podcast, April 23, 2018, https://gretchenrubin.com/podcast/little-happier-working-is-a -form-of-procrastination/.

Chapter 5: Unlabel Yourself

1. Stephen R. Covey, *The 7 Habits of Highly Effective People* (Simon & Schuster, 1989).

Chapter 6: Define Your Own Needs

1. Ed Hoffman, ed., *Future Visions: The Unpublished Papers of Abraham Maslow* (Sage, 1996).

2. A. H. Maslow, "A Theory of Human Motivation," *Psychological Review* 50.4 (1943): 370–396, http://dx.doi.org/10.1037/h0054346.

3. Cindy Blackstock, "The Emergence of the Breath of Life Theory," *Journal of Social Work Values and Ethics* 8.1 (2011): 1–11.

4. Sheila Johnson, *Walk Through Fire* (Simon & Schuster, 2023).

Chapter 8: What Is Believing?

1. Daniel B. Murray and Scott W. Teare, "Probability of a Tossed Coin Landing on Edge," *Physical Review E* 48.4 (1993): 2547, https://doi.org/10.1103/PhysRevE.48.2547.
2. Statistics Canada, "What Are the Chances?" September 2, 2022, https://www.statcan.gc.ca/o1/en/plus/1707-what-are-chances.
3. Jessica Grose, "Why Parents Can't Quit the Elite College Arms Race," *New York Times*, December 6, 2023, https://www.nytimes.com/2023/12/06/opinion/college-grades-parents-students.html.

Chapter 9: Trust Yourself to Fall

1. Daniel Corral, and Shana K. Carpenter, "Long-Term Hypercorrection, Return Errors, and the Transfer of Learning in the Classroom," *Journal of Applied Research in Memory and Cognition* 12.2 (2023): 208–229, https://psycnet.apa.org/doi/10.1037/mac0000048; Janet Metcalfe and David B. Miele, "Hypercorrection of High Confidence Errors: Prior Testing Both Enhances Delayed Performance and Blocks the Return of the Errors," *Journal of Applied Research in Memory and Cognition* 3.3 (2014): 189–197, https://psycnet.apa.org/doi/10.1016/j.jarmac.2014.04.001.
2. Srinwanti H. Chaudhury, Nitika Garg, and Zixi Jiang, "The Curious Case of Threat-Awe: A Theoretical and Empirical Reconceptualization," *Emotion* 22.7 (2022): 1653–1669, https://psycnet.apa.org/doi/10.1037/emo0000984.

Chapter 10: Feel Safe Within

1. Gallup, *State of the Global Workplace: 2024 Report,* Gallup Inc., 2024.
2. Edgar H. Schein, "How Can Organizations Learn Faster? The Challenge of Entering the Green Room," *MIT Sloan Management Review* 34.2 (1993): 85.
3. James Baldwin, *The Fire Next Time* (Vintage, 2013).

Chapter 13: What Is Doing?

1. Martin Luther King Jr., "I've Been To the Mountaintop," March 18, 1968, address delivered at Bishop Charles Mason Temple, https://kinginstitute.stanford.edu/ive-been-mountaintop.

Chapter 14: Love the Game

1. Baxter Holmes, "Misses Add Up to Big Part of Kobe's Legacy," ESPN, November 12, 2014, https://www.espn.com/blog/los-angeles/lakers/post/_/id/40363/misses-add-up-to-big-part-of-kobes-legacy.
2. Kobe Bryant, *The Mamba Mentality* (Farrar, Straus And Giroux, 2018).
3. George T. Doran, "There's a S.M.A.R.T. Way to Write Management's Goals and Objectives," *Management Review* 70.11 (1981): 35–36.

Chapter 15: Throw Rocks with Strangers

1. Peter J. Fadde and Gary A. Klein, "Deliberate Performance: Accelerating Expertise in Natural Settings," *Performance Improvement* 49.9 (2010): 5–14, https://doi.org/10.1002/pfi.20175.
2. Mark R. Nieuwenstein et al., "On Making the Right Choice: A Meta-Analysis and Large-Scale Replication Attempt of the Unconscious Thought Advantage," *Judgment and Decision Making* 10.1 (2015): 1–17, https://psycnet.apa.org/doi/10.1017/S1930297500003144.

Chapter 16: Do What You're Doing

1. Alex Kerai, "Cell Phone Usage Statistics: Mornings Are for Notifications," Reviews.org, July 21, 2023, https://www.reviews.org/mobile/cell-phone-addiction/; "Americans Don't Want to Unplug from Phones While on Vacation, Despite Latest Digital Detox Trend," Asurion, December 5, 2018, https://www.asurion.com/press-releases/americans-dont-want-to-unplug-from-phones-while-on-vacation-despite-latest-digital-detox-trend/.
2. Dave Crenshaw, *The Myth of Multitasking: How "Doing It All" Gets Nothing Done* (Mango Media, 2021).
3. Jia-Qiong Xie et al., "The Association Between Excessive Social Media Use and Distraction: An Eye Movement Tracking Study," *Information & Management* 58.2 (2021): 103415, https://doi.org/10.1016/j.im.2020.103415.
4. Mihaly Csikszentmihalyi, *Creativity: Flow and the Psychology of Discovery and Invention* (Harper, 1996).

Chapter 17: Taking the Right Course

1. Daniel Pink, *Drive: The Surprising Truth About What Motivates Us* (Penguin, 2009).

Chapter 19: Be the Mirror

1. Sarah J. Donovan, C. Dominik Güss, and Dag Naslund, "Improving Dynamic Decision Making Through Training and Self-Reflection," *Judgment and Decision Making* 10.4 (2015): 284–295.
2. Miles M. Yang, Yucheng Zhang, and Feifei Yang, "How a Reflection Intervention Improves the Effect of Learning Goals on Performance Outcomes in a Complex Decision-Making Task," *Journal of Business and Psychology* 33 (2018): 579–593, https://doi.org/10.1007/s10869-017-9510-0.
3. Jane So et al., "The Psychology of Appraisal: Specific Emotions and Decision-Making," *Journal of Consumer Psychology* 25.3 (2015): 359–371, https://doi.org/10.1016/j.jcps.2015.04.003.
4. Ruth Helyer, "Learning Through Reflection: The Critical Role of Reflection in Work-Based Learning (WBL)," *Journal of Work-Applied Management* 7.1 (2015): 15–27, https://www.emerald.com/insight/content/doi/10.1108/JWAM-10-2015-003/full/html.

Chapter 20: Shimmer like Gold

1. David Kindy, "The Accidental Invention of Play-Doh," *Smithsonian Magazine*, November 12, 2019, https://www.smithsonianmag.com/innovation/accidental-invention-play-doh-180973527/.

Appendix: Raise Their Roof

1. Sophia Obrecht, "From Childhood Dreams to Paralympic Victory: Lauren Rowles Shares the Ups and Downs of Life After Crossing the Finish Line," *GamePlan A*, Adidas, archived August 3, 2022, at https://web.archive.org/web/20220803222421/https://www.gameplan-a.com/2022/08/from-childhood-dreams-to-paralympic-victory-lauren-rowles-shares-the-ups-and-downs-of-life-after-crossing-the-finish-line/.